PHALLÓS

Bronzino, Duke of Urbino (Page 165)

THORKIL VANGGAARD

PHALLÓS

A SYMBOL AND ITS HISTORY IN THE MALE WORLD

Translated from the Danish
by the Author

INTERNATIONAL UNIVERSITIES PRESS, INC.
NEW YORK

FIRST PUBLISHED IN DENMARK UNDER THE TITLE PHALLÓS
© 1969 BY THORKIL VANGGAARD
THIS TRANSLATION FIRST PUBLISHED IN GREAT BRITAIN 1972
© 1972 BY THORKIL VANGGAARD

INTERNATIONAL UNIVERSITIES PRESS, INC.

Library of Congress Catalogue Card Number: 72-80553

ISBN 0-8236-4135-X

Contents

CONCLUSION

Illustrations

The illustrations appear at the end of the book

Preface

A number of persons have been of great help to me during my work with this book.

The Director General of Museums and Antiquities in Denmark, Professor P. V. Glob, and the Professor of Penal Law at the University of Copenhagen, Knud Waaben, both gave me most willingly the benefit of their expertise. They supplied me with useful information, and checked the material I had collected, putting in considerable time and effort, and showing the greatest interest. I would hardly have dared to publish the chapters in question without their invaluable help. In addition, Professor Glob kindly gave me permission to include in this book a number of photographs taken by him.

The Keeper of Prints and Drawings at The Royal Museum of Fine Arts, Copenhagen, Erik Fischer, M.A., Henrik Neiiendam, M.A., and Ole J. Rafaelsen, M.D., checked over the whole manuscript and Professor Mogens Westergaard over a part of it. As a result of the thoroughness of these friends of mine I received a great number of valuable critical suggestions.

My son, Jens Henrik Vanggaard, M.A., followed my work in a similar way. In particular he carefully checked the translations from the Greek and Latin to ensure their accuracy.

Miss Jola Hemmes was responsible for all the secretarial work. It is difficult to find words to convey my appreciation of the skill, care, and effort she devoted to my work.

Mrs Grace Goldin of Yale went over part of my translation, and Mrs Barbara Sullivan in London over the whole of it, correcting it most carefully. I am deeply indebted to them both. To all I offer my best thanks.

Introduction

This is a book about a symbol and its history.

Natural phenomena, whether within human beings or outside them, turn into symbols when they assume meanings and roles other than those they possessed in the first place. A symbol always has many meanings and may appear to have one or several at the same time. When it is assuming several different roles at one time, it is quite usual for some to be mutually incompatible when judged by the standards of ordinary logic. These general, abstract statements will be illustrated by more concrete examples below and in the following chapters.

Parts of the body may take on a symbolic meaning. Thus, the erect penis turns into a symbol when its meanings go beyond the directly biological, and when the roles it plays mainly serve goals other than passion and procreation. The penis in its symbolic capacity is named *Phallus*.

Living in a civilization set and defined by life in the big cities of Europe and Northern America, we have a different attitude towards symbols from that of the people in many other cultures. For them, symbols are interwoven with the thoughts, feelings, and doings of their daily life. Symbols are unavoidable, indispensable, and just as real as mountains, the ocean, animals, or human beings. For instance, the slaughtering at the great festivals in ancient Scandinavia contained a symbolic meaning along with its purely practical one. If the slaughtering were not performed according to the correct ritual and at the right time of the year, the new year would be ill fated. Similarly, the ceremonial drinking of the toast at the Yuletide festival was of great significance;

the law prescribed punishment for any yeoman who did not use
for his beer-making a measure of grain proportionate to the size
of his farm and household. If he used less he not only cheated
his men, he endangered the common welfare, since the course of
the year, the solidarity—or 'Peace'*—between kinsmen, and
even the well-being of the country as a whole, was imperilled if
the toast was not drunk with a sufficient quantity of beer and in
the prescribed way. When the drinking-horn was passed round
'for year and peace' (this being a literal translation of the old
Scandinavian formula) a ritual was enacted which had importance
far beyond the pleasure of convivial drinking with kinsmen and
friends at the great festival.

The slaughterings and the toasts were truly symbolic. Their
meanings went beyond the ostensible ones, so that the toast, for
instance, was not just an expression of good wishes; it had a real
influence on the forthcoming year and on people's relations with
each other. The course of events would alter if the toast was not
drunk in the correct way.

The same thing happened when, in the seventh century B.C., a
Dorian nobleman through his phallus transferred to a boy the
essence of his best qualities as a man. Since erotic pleasure was
subordinated to a more important aim this was a genuinely
symbolic act, the aim being to make of the boy a man with
strength, a sense of duty, eloquence, cleverness, generosity,
courage, and all the other noble virtues. Again, the act was not
symbolic in the sense that we use the word, to denote something
which seems to be what in reality it is not. For the Dorian, a real
event took place; through the pederastic act the grown man's
valuable qualities, which were as these people saw it incorporated
in his phallus, were transferred to the boy. With the help of
Apollo the older man could convey his noble manhood to the
youth.

* 'Peace' in the old Norse language had nothing to do with the absence of war. The
concept was limited to the relationship between kinsmen and those united under the same
thegn or king.

Something parallel happened in New Guinea when a Kiwai Papuan selected a tree which seemed fit for the making of a harpoon shaft. He would then press his phallus against the trunk of the tree so that the harpoon shaft might be straight, strong, and with great power of penetration. He transferred the qualities of his phallus to the tree.[1] This illustrates, as does the previous example, why it is meaningful to use the word 'phallus' instead of the anatomical name 'penis'; the meanings of the roles given to this part of the male body reveal that the primary aim was not the sexual satisfaction of the man who performed the act. For the Dorians, eros between man and boy was a means to higher goals; in the rite of the Papuan it is not possible to find even a trace of sexuality, as the word is usually understood, although he used his sexual organ. The symbolic meaning may be attached to the part of the body itself, or to a picture of it.

Our own relationship to symbols is quite a different matter. Symbols do not possess any equivalent reality in our lives. A few have survived like pale shadows from ancient times, such as the drinking of toasts in Scandinavia. During a formal or even a semi-formal dinner it is the rule — and one which astonishes foreigners—never to take a drink on your own. You raise your wineglass, looking into somebody else's eyes—the lady's on your right or, together with her, into those of some other couple at the table—you drink and again look at each other with a slight nod before putting your glass back on the table. Ladies are not really supposed to take the initiative in drinking. This ceremonial drinking of toasts is the remnant of an ancient and solemn custom. But nobody now believes in all seriousness that the fate of men in this life or of the dead in the next will alter if the toast is not drunk in the proper way. When we call something symbolic we merely mean that it seems to represent what everybody knows it is not in reality; nobody would expect any tangible effects from a symbolic act. Remnants of the attitudes of former times which are still found occasionally are regarded as superstition, even, as a rule, by the very people who adopt these attitudes. Our daily actions are not accompanied by symbolic acts which we consider essential for their accomplishment. To most of us, rituals performed by symbolic figures do not appear as reality endowed with a cosmic and personal significance.

This difference in attitude towards symbols can be seen clearly when we compare ourselves with so-called primitive peoples who are still able to lead their own lives unaffected by our self-confident interference.

Our attitude towards symbols has had certain important effects. In the first place, a spontaneous understanding of symbols has been lost. It is safe to say 'lost', because we may be sure our forefathers had it. When Freud became famous through revealing the meaning of symbols and their role in our lives, his achievement did not lie, like so many discoveries in the natural sciences, in the attainment of new knowledge. Freud's contribution as far as symbols are concerned is to be regarded as a rediscovery, laboriously acquired through intellectual analysis, of something which previously was—and in other cultures still is—given knowledge. Freud's accomplishment is not less because of that, naturally. How the field of our human understanding was narrowed when symbols were chased out of the realms of our consciousness is nowhere more clearly to be seen than in that branch of science which is particularly concerned with symbols: the history of religions. When sex-symbolism appears it is almost always classified as a fertility cult. And the phallic symbol is thus categorized in a way seemingly simple and rational, which, moreover, conforms to many of the most important prejudices of our civilization. I shall try to show the limitations of this view.

In line with this, representations of 'The Sacred Marriage'— copulation between god and goddess—are seen by many as just an expression of the fertility cult. However, when coming face to face with a statuette of an Indian or Tibetan Shiva and Shakti in standing copulation, even without knowledge of the iconography of these figures one must perceive this to be the representation of much more than an act of fertility.

Our knowledge of ourselves and of human beings in general is limited in other respects, too, compared with that of the so-called primitives. For decades science denied that human beings possessed natural propensities for exerting power, for dominating their fellows and taking their possessions and even their lives from them. We could not believe in the existence in ourselves of an independent aggressive drive. Aggressive behaviour had to be understood as a reaction to threat or frustration; provided people were given what they needed and were not frightened, they would not be aggressive. This is not primarily a scientific point of view. It expresses in the form of scientific theory a belief in the fundamental goodness of man. This belief, which was created by us relatively recently, has led to the concept of God as pure, unlimited, unconditional goodness. In many quarters the fear of God has been dropped from the Christian message. Upbringing and teaching have been profoundly and seriously affected by this concept of man, which is also grotesquely expressed in the fact that nowadays most countries have a government department only for the defence of the nation. Nobody admits to attacking somebody else without provocation; it is only the other man who does!

However, as early as 1920 Freud was postulating the existence of an autonomous aggressive drive. Unfortunately he placed this new concept within a not very useful theoretical framework derived from physics, and formed the hypothesis of the Death Instinct. Later some of his pupils — the foremost among them being Heinz Hartmann and his collaborators in New York — pursued the matter purely from the clinical standpoint and contributed significantly to a clarification of the theory of aggression.[2] Deductions derived from the study of animal behaviour followed parallel lines, and although in some quarters diehard resistance remains, the concept of an autonomous aggressive drive has now been firmly established. In recent years we have seen the publication of highly informative popular books by Lorenz[3] and Storr,[4] books in which autonomous aggression is regarded not simply as a regrettable, inevitable evil, but as an indispensable radical in human nature, without which society would not exist and survival would be impossible.

By a radical—a term I shall often use—I mean a factor rooted in human nature, for instance a drive and its preformed modes of possible discharge. I speak of the sexual drive as a radical, for instance, and of heterosexual and homosexual ways of discharge as radicals. A radical is something inherent in humans, something which, in everybody and at all times, exerts a powerful pressure, and which therefore has to be dealt with either by being given discharge in some form, or by being suppressed in one way or another.

No people but the Europeans and Americans could have hit upon the idea of denying the existence of a primary aggressive element in human nature; nor is it likely that a god who is autocratic and at the same time purely good could have been invented except by us. Changes emerging from the recognition of the existence of the aggressive drive (by no means generally accepted) are to be regarded as attempts by way of the intellect to regain a lost insight.

Our understanding of the aggressive meaning and roles of sex-symbolism in life is correspondingly poor. In this book these topics will be discussed at length.

There is still another basic element which is usually barred from our field of consciousness. It is the homosexual radical. Its nature, what it meant in different cultures, and the fate it has met with in our own, is an important theme in this work.

Erotica—that is, sexual phenomena having emotional and

sensual pleasure as their main aims, heterosexually, homosexually, or in other ways—lie outside my subject and will be mentioned only incidentally. Accordingly, the aesthetic-erotic pederasty in Hellenistic Rome or in Islam of the Abbassides—the latter depicted so vividly throughout *The Arabian Nights*—is also outside my topic. The fertility aspect of the phallus symbol and of 'The Sacred Marriage', *hieros gamos*, is so well known and so frequently treated that I will not elaborate too much on it here.

Emphasis will be laid upon other symbolic meanings of the phallus, among them the aggressive ones, and those occurring in a homosexual context with men otherwise heterosexually oriented.

I shall now characterize the concept of homosexuality as I intend to use it.[5] The word homosexual as applied to men may have at least three different meanings.

1. To refer to homosexual feelings, fantasies, impulses, and acts among men who are normal in their erotic attitude towards women.

2. To refer to a group of men, a small percentage of the population, who are the true homosexuals according to the common usage of the word. These men feel attracted homosexually and are potent in homosexual relationships, but they do not feel erotic attraction to women, and they are not genitally potent with them. Men of this group are distinguished from the first mainly by their relationship to women. In this book they are referred to as inversely homosexual or inverse.

3. To refer to the so-called transvestites—men, that is, who want to be women, to dress like women, and be treated as women by heterosexual men. Often they have no wish for genital stimulation or for achieving orgasm. Men who would rather have their genitals removed by surgery belong to this group.*

In most cases it is easy to distinguish between these types.

---

* I do not here distinguish between transvestism and transsexualism because these conditions are outside the subject of this book.

B

However, as is the case everywhere in human typology, transitional forms are seen, although not in great numbers.

The homosexual relationships mentioned in this book belong exclusively to the first group. The particular problems of the two other groups will not be discussed.

In our civilization phallic symbolism and the homosexual radical do not openly manifest themselves in average adult males. They are not visibly integrated in our patterns of action and our conscious thoughts and feelings. Nevertheless, homosexual phenomena occur in our world more frequently than is officially recognized, particularly among boys and youths. Even more essential, however, the absence of overt homosexuality in the conscious daily life of ordinary adult males does not mean that with us, in contrast to men in the rest of the world, the homosexual radical is lacking. Beneath the threshold of consciousness it is present in any man, handled in different ways, determined by our particular pattern of civilization, unfolding its effects in disguised forms. This will be shown in subsequent chapters by concrete examples including those taken from clinical experience.

The nature and significance of the phallic symbol and of homosexuality will be illustrated and explained by reference to our knowledge about life in ancient Greece and within the ancient Norse culture, compared with modern clinical experience. This will be supplemented by some observations on the behaviour of the higher mammals — the primates — made in the last few decades. Some aspects of life in the Near East throughout history are also taken into consideration. After describing the clash between Judeo-Christianity and the rest of the Hellenistic world, I will try to follow phallic symbolism in some of its forms down through European culture into our present European–American civilization. In this context the role of sexual symbols as signals of dominance and submission will be exhaustively discussed, and related to personal relationships and social systems ancient and modern.

To avoid making the book too lengthy and complicated I have not treated fantasies of the phallic woman — illustrated for instance by Greek androgynous statues — fantasies which are of great importance in the development of all men. I have also omitted any reference to the significance of phallic symbolism during infantile female development and its cultic importance for grown women in many cultures. Nor do I deal with the symbolic meanings and roles of the female genitals, or with homosexuality in normal women. The latter, incidentally, has never attracted much attention anywhere — one of the obvious signs of vast differences between the sexes.

Although I have chosen to deal almost exclusively with the meaning and role of the phallic symbol between men, I should like to emphasize that it is not because this context is more important than the heterosexual one, but because it *is* important, and it is less known. For the same reason I have laid more stress on the aggressive rather than the erotic aspects of phallic symbolism and homosexuality.

NOTES

1. Gunnar Landtman, *The Kiwai Papuans of British New Guinea* (London, 1927), p. 120.
2. H. Hartmann, E. Kris, and R. Loewenstein, 'Notes on the Theory of Aggression', *The Psychoanalytic Study of the Child*, III–IV (London, 1950).
3. Konrad Lorenz, *On Aggression* (London, 1963).
4. Anthony Storr, *Human Aggression* (London, 1968).
5. Thorkil Vanggaard, 'Normal homoseksualitet og homoseksuel inversion' (*Ugeskrift for Læger*, 1962), 124, p. 1427 ff.

BOOK I

We must accept that for the Hellenes the phallus symbolized the full force of manliness, not just procreative power. This would apply to gods as well as to mortals.

ULRICH VON WILAMOWITZ-MOELLENDORFF

I

Paiderastia

'Invoking the Delphic Apollo, I, Crimon, here copulated with a boy, son of Bathycles.' This inscription in the Dorian–Greek dialect is hewn in the rock wall beside the temple of Apollo Carneius, on the little island of Thera (Santorin) in the Aegean Sea north of Crete.[1] Apollo Carneius was a Dorian god. The inscription dates from the seventh century B.C. The Dorian verb *óphein* is commonly used to describe copulation with women, corresponding to the Latin *coire*. There are numerous similar inscriptions in the rock, all following a common formula: 'Here X copulated with Y.' Both X and Y are given in the masculine; X is in the nominative, and Y, which designates a boy, is in the accusative. So these inscriptions are proclamations of fulfilled *paiderastia*,* a word derived from *pais*, a boy, and *erastēs*, a lover, this word being a derivative of the word *eran* – to love.

When Crimon issues a declaration to the world in this way about his relationship to the son of Bathycles, it cannot be an expression of coarseness, obscenity, or obdurate vice, as we would consider it to be if a man were to proclaim that he had celebrated anal coitus with a boy. The sacred place and the name of Apollo

---

* When dealing with the ancient Greek world I shall use the word *paiderastia* or *paiderasty* in order to avoid, if possible, the connotation automatically clinging to the latinized, modern term pederasty.

make it plain that, on the contrary, we are being told about a sacred act, steeped in solemnity and honour.*

I shall return to this later to explain its meaning. It is introduced here as testimony from the Dorian world of the seventh century to the predominant attitude towards paiderastic relationships in archaic and classical times, that is, in the period from about 750–300 B.C. The grown men in these relationships were fully potent with women, and the young partners developed the same dual attitude. So for Greek men at this time sexual relations with women and men were not a matter of either/or. These men could be conscious of both homosexual and heterosexual inclinations and could express them in action without coming into conflict with themselves or their surroundings. This trait in the Greek way of life should not be confused with the more tolerant attitude now shown towards inverse homosexuals (see the definition on page 17).

These conditions which prevailed in ancient Greece fit in with the assumption of psychoanalytical theory, supported by the experience of many decades: that a homosexual radical is inherent in the nature of all males—not just those who are inverse, but also the vast majority of men who are not. This testimony comes down to us from a culture which we cannot simply label primitive as we tend to do people whose style of life is essentially different from ours. On the contrary, we admire the Greeks, we feel that we are in debt to them culturally, philosophically, and scientifically, and it is a widespread belief that our democracy was formed by following the Greek pattern. In addition, the Greeks left us so much information about their actions and thoughts that we know the essential things about them with a considerable degree of certainty.

This being so, I shall review the material available to us con-

---

* Philologically this is reflected in the following: in connection with the word *beinein*, meaning in ordinary daily language to copulate, the lexicographer Hesycius, fifth century A.D., tells us that *opyiein*, Attic dialect for the Dorian *óphein*, means to copulate *according to the law*. In legal terms, it is used to mean the marriage act (see Liddell and Scott).

cerning Greek paiderasty, and try to determine what conclusions
we may come to about its nature and its meaning.

First a few remarks about the kind of sources we have at our
disposal. Some are from the period about which they give us
information. Such is the case with the seventh-century inscriptions from the island of Thera and inscriptions and paintings on
vases of the sixth and fifth century B.C. We have literary sources
also, dating with certainty from these same periods: historical
narratives like the *Anabasis* of Xenophon and philosophical
writings such as those of Plato which unmistakably deal with the
forms of life of their own time. Poets like Theognis of the sixth
century, Pindar and the tragic poets Aeschylus, Sophocles, and
Euripides from the fifth century B.C., and the comic playwright
Aristophanes, all refer to paiderasty. Finally, we have the literature of Hellenistic times — the period from *c.* 300 B.C. to *c.* A.D. 400
— based on sources now lost to us, the most important being
Plutarch, first to second century A.D., and Strabo, first century
A.D. These authors are commonly thought reliable.

From Attica we have a great number of vases of high artistic
quality — black-figure vases from the sixth century B.C. and red-
figure vases from the fifth century. A typical inscription on many
of these vases, repeated again and again, is: 'The boy is beautiful'
(*ho pais kalós*, or *ho deina kalós*). In this context *kalós*, beautiful,
has a decidedly erotic connotation. These vases are generally
called '*Kalós* vases', owing to their inscriptions. They were gifts
of love from a lover — *erastēs* — to a beloved boy — *erōmenos* or
paidicá. Fig. 1 shows a black-figure vase of this kind, *c.* 550 B.C.
Its decoration depicts in the most direct way a paiderastic situation: a man is addressing himself urgently to a boy; his size and
powerful body, in contrast to the smaller, slender boy, clearly
identifies him as the older of the two. The man has the beard
of the grown Greek, and his phallus is strong and erect — he is
phallic, as we say — while the boy is beardless and without phallic
attribute. The man extends a wreath towards the youth who has

a wreath in his own hand; in the iconography of these vases the wreath is a sign of love. The man holds a big dog on a leash. The dog strains upward towards the boy. In Greek iconography the dog has phallic significance; the word for dog, *kyōn*, is used to denote the male genital, and in this picture the lover's dog is probably there to emphasize his phallic power.

This painting proves the vase to be a token of love, and sensual love at that, given by an *erastēs* to an *erōmenos* in a paiderastic relationship. One feature typical of a Greek relationship of this kind is strongly emphasized in the painting: the older powerful man is taking the initiative; he is the giver, while the youth receives. This is conveyed by the contrast between the two figures and is highlighted by the fact that the *erastēs* is so markedly phallic while the young *erōmenos* is without phallic attribute.

Solon, who reformed Athenian society shortly after 600 B.C. and probably lived until about 550, laid down rules for paiderasty among his laws, thus testifying not only to the common occurrence of this phenomenon, but to the great importance ascribed to it. Under the threat of severe punishment he forbade slaves to have sexual intercourse with free boys, nor were they permitted to rub the boys with oil after the exercises in the *palaestra* (the place of exercise surrounded by colonnades in the gymnasium).[2] It is clear from several sources that rubbing with oil was often the introduction to a paiderastic relationship. Plutarch adds the comment that by these rules Solon placed paiderasty 'in the category of what was honourable and worthy, thus in a way prompting the worthy to that which he forbade the unworthy'.[3]

Solon was not only a giver of laws, he was also a poet, and in a preserved fragment, quoted by Plutarch,[4] he speaks with enthusiasm about paiderasty:

> Till he loves a lad in the flower of youth,
> bewitched by thighs and by sweet lips.

But Solon praises the love of women as well:

'Precious are for me now the works of Aphrodite ... that make men merry.'[5] He counsels in favour of marriage: in the fifth seven-year period of life, he says, a man ought to marry and beget offspring[6] and, he adds, happy is the man who has dear children.[7]

This last sentiment is also expressed by Theognis[8] in about the middle of the sixth century B.C. His many verses addressed to his young friend Cyrnus may be seen as a poetic counterpart to the contemporary vase painting illustrated in Figure 1. Among Theognis' many expressions of what can best be described as a zest for paiderasty is this one, 'Happy the man who loves while he takes his exercise and who, when he goes home [i.e. from the *palaestra*], sleeps to the end of the day with a handsome boy.'[9]

Paiderasty is mentioned in the *Anabasis* of Xenophon as being part of ordinary daily life. The *Anabasis* is Xenophon's report of how, in 401 B.C., he led home from Persia ten thousand Greeks who had been mercenaries for Cyrus the Younger. The march through Asia Minor was so arduous and dangerous that to make the journey easier it became necessary to compel the soldiers to throw away most of their booty. Xenophon describes how he had the soldiers lined up in a mountain pass where it was possible to supervise them to ensure that the orders had been obeyed. If it was found that a soldier had kept something expressly against orders, it was taken away from him. The soldiers put up with this, 'except where a man had smuggled in with him a handsome boy or a woman whom he had set his heart on'[10] — boy and woman mentioned in the same breath! He goes on to relate how Clearchus, a Spartan, one of the three generals who had originally led the ten thousand, enjoyed fighting so much that he was just as willing to spend his money on warfare as on a *paidicá* or some other entertainment.[11] In another of his books[12] Xenophon says that men and boys in Boeotia and other Greek states 'were living together like married couples'.

Paiderasty is common practice among the gods and heroes of the Hellenes—and it should be remembered that important patterns in the life of a people always appear in their myths and legends. Zeus abducted Ganymede because he was overwhelmed by love for him; transforming himself into an eagle, he seized the boy, flew with him to Olympus and made him his *erōmenos* and the cup-bearer of the gods. Figure 2 shows a vase painting of Ganymede, from the fifth century B.C. The handsome youth is holding a hoop, and in his other hand he carries a cock. Like the dog, the cock is a phallic representation—figures of a phallus often had the wings and legs of a cock. Iconographically the cock is a token of love, like the wreath in Figure 1, given by an *erastēs* to his *erōmenos*. Nothing blameworthy could possibly be attached to paiderasty in the minds of people who had a myth as this about their supreme god.

Pelops, the hero after whom the Peloponnese was named, was the *erōmenos* of Poseidon. Pindar relates this myth in his first *Olympian Ode*, written in honour of Hiero, absolute ruler of Syracuse. Hiero's horse, Pherenicus, had won the horse races at the Olympian games in 476 B.C. In his eulogy Pindar likens Hiero to Pelops, because by the help of Poseidon Pelops won a race against King Oenomaus, thereby gaining the hand of Oenomaus' daughter, Hippodameia. Pindar relates the story underlying Poseidon's help to Pelops: overcome by his desire for Pelops, Poseidon abducted the boy and kept him for a time as his *erōmenos*. Later, when the first growth of beard began to darken Pelops' cheeks, Poseidon sent him back to the human world. Pelops then wanted to take a wife, and set his heart on winning Hippodameia. However, Hippodameia's father, Oenomaus, demanded that her suitors stake their lives in a race against his horses. Already he had killed thirteen suitors who had been bested by the king's four-in-hand. In the dark of the night Pelops then walked to the grey sea and invoked the god of the heavy trident, commencing thus: 'Look you, Poseidon, if ever you have had joy of my love and of the Cyprian's* sweet gifts …'[13]. In the same ode Pindar also refers to Zeus' relationship with Ganymede.

Clearly it flattered Hiero to be compared with the *erōmenos* of Poseidon. Immediately we feel how far distant these people were from our own civilization and its attitudes, if a mighty ruler could appreciate such a comparison. It is interesting to note, by the way, that after his love relationship with Poseidon, Pelops risked his life to win a woman — later he was to have six sons by her — and that his *erastēs* helped him to get her. This reflects the circumstances of ordinary life. When a young man came of age he married. In the choice of a proper wife, the *erastēs* might play an important role, having, as we shall see, far-reaching responsibilities and duties towards his *erōmenos*. Again it appears that the Hellenes feared no conflict between homosexuality and heterosexuality. Our attitude — that they tend to be mutually exclusive and to thrive only at each other's expense — was unknown to the Greeks. The difference between Greek paiderastia and today's notions of homosexuality emerges clearly in this.

Pindar tells us in his own words that he himself practised paiderasty. He wrote an ode in honour of his *erōmenos*, Theoxenus, son of Hegesilaus of Tenedus. In the ode he says that at the sight of the youth's young limbs he melted like bees' wax in the sunshine; at Tenedus he was overcome by the son of Hegesilaus, whom Grace herself had fostered.[14]

It is further told of Pelops that later he had a son, Chrysippus. On a visit to Pelops, Laius, the king of Thebes, fell in love with Chrysippus while teaching the boy the art of managing a four-in-hand. Driven by untameable desire he abducted the boy. In his wrath and outrage Pelops cursed Laius and his kin.[15]

It is known that Euripides wrote a tragedy, *Chrysippus*, dealing with the boy's abduction and Pelops' curse. Plutarch refers to Laius' kidnapping of Chrysippus and quotes a line of verse, probably from this play.[16] Plato gives further evidence that the myth

* i.e. Aphrodite.

was commonly known in the fifth and fourth centuries B.C.[17] As a result of the curse, Laius was killed by his son Oedipus when they met and quarrelled on the road from Thebes to Delphi, unaware that they were father and son. Oedipus then married Jocasta, ignorant of the fact that she was the widow of Laius and his own mother. Sophocles describes the tragic outcome in *Oedipus Rex* and *Oedipus at Colonus*. Hans Licht[18] rightly emphasizes that it would be a naïve misunderstanding to assume that Pelops cursed Laius because of his homosexual relationship to the boy. Laius' crime was that he took the boy without the father's consent, thereby violating the rights and duties of host and guest. In the myth of Ganymede it is expressly stated that Zeus had to pay dearly to the boy's father, King Trōs, to right the wrong he had done him.

Apollo had relationships with many youths, the first of whom was Hyacinthus; the summer festival *Hyacinthia* commemorated this relationship.[19] Heracles had an immense appetite for women — he is said to have lain with all fifty daughters of Thesbius in one night. However, he also had many paiderastic relationships, the most famous with Iolaus whose grave still existed at Thebes as an object of worship in the time of Pausanias (second to third century A.D.). As with Poseidon and Pelops, this relationship shows how the *erastēs* would lead the young man into marriage when the latter was of the right age. Heracles even gave his own wife, Megara, to Iolaus.[20] This conflict-free sexual dualism is also testified to in another legend about Heracles, who used his powers of healing to save the life of Alcestis. He did so to please Admetus who loved his wife dearly. Admetus, also, had been the *erōmenos* of Heracles and had a similar relationship to Apollo.[21]

Dionysus was himself a phallic god—one of his names was Phalēs. It is told of him that Polymnus showed him the way to Hades; in return Dionysus agreed to give himself to Polymnus in a love relationship. In one version of the myth Dionysus does so before the descent. In another Polymnus dies. Dionysus buries

him, carves a phallus of wood, sticks it into the earth above the
grave and sits down upon it, thus fulfilling his promise of anal
copulation with the dead man.[22]

In the works of the tragic poets the theme of paiderasty appears
again and again, mostly in tragedies known only from fragments
and quoted by authors of later times to whom they were still
available in their entirety. In 467 B.C., Aeschylus' tetralogy *Laius*,
Oedipus, *Seven Against Thebes*, and the satyric drama *The Sphinx*,
were put on the stage. Only *Seven Against Thebes* is preserved.
However, there is reason to believe that *Laius* was about the
conflict between Laius and Pelops, with the curse serving as the
starting point for the next tragedy, *Oedipus*. We also have a fragment from another Aeschylean tragedy, *The Myrmidons*, dealing
with the death of Patroclus and Achilles' grief, which reads:
'You did not appreciate my admiration of your thighs, un-
grateful you were for our many kisses.'[23]
The pronoun designating the person to whom this is directed
is in the masculine. The quotation is cited by Plutarch as a parallel
to the lines by Solon, mentioned above,[24] and the words probably
belonged to the speech delivered by Achilles at the pyre of
Patroclus. So it was a reproach to the dead man because he went
into the battle, which proved fatal, against the wish of Achilles.
It is interesting to observe that the *Iliad* is silent on the subject
of paiderasty. The conception of the relationship between Achilles
and Patroclus as a paiderastic one (see also Plato, *Symposium* 179)
may have come into being at a later date.*
The Laius–Chrysippus legend also formed the basis of a lost
tragedy by Euripides. It is said that this tragedy was a declaration
of love by Euripides, identifying himself with Laius, for Agaton
in the figure of Chrysippus. It was this same Agaton, himself an
eminent tragic poet, who appeared in Plato's *Symposium* as well

* In a discussion of the origins of the Homeric material, this might be one argument for
the view that essentially it dates from before the Dorian invasion.

as in the *Thesmophoriazusae* by Aristophanes. He was famous for his extraordinary gifts and beauty.[25]

Athenaeus speaks in no uncertain terms of the affinity of Aeschylus and Sophocles to paiderasty. Writing of 'Songs in honour of favourite boys' he says that the love of boys was so far from being regarded as mean 'that even great poets like Aeschylus and Sophocles introduced such themes of love on the stage in their tragedies — first that of Achilles and Patroclus, then that of the boys in *Niobe*.'[26]

I hope that sufficient documentary evidence has been given to show that paiderasty was cultivated by heterosexually normal men in ancient Greece, where it did not presuppose an inversely homosexual type of personality. It was not considered a transgression, to be tolerated, nor was it felt to betoken any laxity in moral standards; it was a natural part of the life-style of the best of men, reflected in the stories of the gods and heroes of the people. We owe our appreciation of this to Bethe's distinguished paper of 1907[27] (this paper, incidentally, has gone peculiarly unnoticed; a striking fact, since Bethe was a philologist of high repute whose works were not otherwise overlooked).

Bethe says that in the Dorian world paiderasty was a central factor in the upbringing of boys and youths; it was a means of imparting to them the best qualities of the Dorian nobleman. According to Bethe, the implication of the Thera inscription announcing Crimon's copulation with the son of Bathycles at the temple of Apollo is that the boy is thereby given noble manhood — *aretē*.

Bethe supports his theses with historical material from those parts of Greece which were dominated by the Dorian way of life. Before we take a closer look at his ideas, it might be as well to differentiate between the three tribes constituting the Greek people in archaic and classical times. In the second millennium B.C. the Greek mainland and the islands were inhabited by

Ionians and Aeolians who had developed a magnificent palace-culture, mainly centred in Mycenae, Tiryns, and Pylos in the Peloponnese, the Acropolis of Attica and Knossos in Crete. In about 1200 B.C. — half a century after the Troy of the *Iliad* had been destroyed — a Greek-speaking people from the north-west, the Dorians, began to invade the Greek mainland, ravaging, plundering, and laying waste the land. In the course of the following two centuries, roughly from 1200 to 1000 B.C., they conquered the whole of the Greek mainland. They came in several waves, the first crossing the Corinthian Gulf to the west coast of the Peloponnese in about 1200. Here they destroyed the palace of Pylos, which may have been ruled by Nestor of the *Iliad* at a somewhat earlier time. The excavations of Blegen show how the palace was overrun, looted, and burned literally in a matter of moments. Later Dorian invasions forced their way via Thessaly, Boeotia, and the Isthmus — the narrow connection between the mainland and the Peloponnese — to Argos and the eastern, middle, and southern parts of the Peloponnese. Thence they proceeded eastward over the Aegean Sea to Crete, Thera, and the southern part of the coast of Asia Minor.* Everywhere they wiped out the Cretan–Mycenaean culture. The castle of Mycenae held out for a long time; it was attacked throughout a whole century before it was finally conquered and burned. However, the Dorians never managed to take the Acropolis of Athens, and it was here that the Ionians and Aeolians, fleeing from the rest of the country, found refuge. Later they proceeded to the northern islands of the Aegean Sea, the Aeolians to Lesbos, among other places, and the Ionians to Asia Minor, colonizing its coast. Subsequently, the Dorians turned to the west and colonized Sicily, founding Syracuse and Acragas (Agrigentum). Hiero, ruler of Syracuse (praised in Pindar's first Olympian Ode, mentioned above), was a Dorian. Xenophon[28] has preserved for us the name of Hiero's *erōmenos*, Dailochus, to whom he was much devoted.

* See Fig. 3.

These Dorians supervised the upbringing of boys with an intensity, severity, and consistency greatly admired by the rest of the Greeks. Everywhere the aim of upbringing was the development of *aret*, a word conveying a common Greek concept of nobility for which we have no precise equivalent in present-day language. (Its meaning is close to the old Norse *hamingja*.) *Aretē* covers a multitude of meanings which, nevertheless, should be seen as an entity. We know the meaning of *aretē* from Homer, from the Spartan poet Tyrtaeus, writing in the seventh century B.C., from Theognis, in the sixth century B.C., and from Pindar. Vilhelm Grønbech* in *Hellas*, vol. 1, and Werner Jaeger in *Paideia*, vol. 1, part 1, give penetrating analyses of the concept of *aretē* as expressing the ideal of Greek nobility — that nobility which was, according to Jaeger,[29] the source of the spiritual culture of Greece and therefore of such importance for our own culture.

Grønbech says of *aretē* that it showed itself as 'the driving force of a man's skill, power, and character'.[30]

It manifested itself in his skill in his use of weapons, in the way he steered his four-in-hand, rode his horse, formed his speech — ingeniously like Odysseus, or tersely like a Spartan; or ran like Achilles, swift of foot. It manifested itself in his power of body and of spirit, and it manifested itself in his character — his courage and steadfastness in battle (the death-wounds of the fallen had to be in front); his hardihood, faithfulness to his duties; his obedience; his power of authority; his sense of solidarity with his fellows and his country; his faithfulness in personal relations; his honesty and integrity, power of judgment, fairness, temperance, generosity, and reliability as a host or a guest.

Aretē is interwoven with honour — *kydos* — and with fame and distinction — *kleos* and *timē*. *Aretē* was inconceivable without nobility testified to by ancestry. Fathers and forefathers were

---

* An eminent Danish religious historian, professor at the University of Copenhagen. Unfortunately few of his books have been translated into English.

invariably enumerated when a man was described. In the Thera-inscription Crimon does not mention the boy by his own name, but as the son of his father, because the father's nobility is the guarantee that the boy is fit to aspire to *aretē*. Our idea of human development as being formed by inheritance and environment—that is, by both natural endowment and upbringing—has its counterpart in the belief of the ancient Greeks that inherit-ance, manifested in a noble ancestry, combined with the right kind of upbringing were preconditions for the acquisition of *aretē*.

It is important to note that qualities of mind and bodily skills went equally to make up the concept of *aretē*; a man's nature showed itself as much in his bodily capacities as in the nobility of his mind. Great *aretē* might emerge equally in the clarity and profundity of his thought, in the steadfastness of his character, or in the strength and nimbleness of his body. Homer says about a certain man that he has 'great *aretē* in the swiftness of his feet, in his actions in battle, and in his mind [*noos*]',[31] and Pindar talks of '*aretē* of the feet'[32] or '*aretē* won by the fist'.[33] Thus we see *aretē* as expressing a view of human nature quite different from ours, unaware, as the Greeks were, of the concept of a dualistic division between mind and body.

So *aretē* was the kernel of the prevailing Greek ideal of nobility depicted both by the Ionian Homer and by the Dorian poets. However, no race in the Greek world pursued this ideal in the upbringing of their young so zealously as the Dorians. The system of upbringing in Sparta and in Crete, for instance, was severe and merciless. Boys had to leave their homes at the age of seven and were enrolled in corps under the leadership of older boys and youths, who were in their turn supervised by older men. The boys lived in barracks and took their meals in a mess-hall like the grown men; the conditions in which they lived were primitive and hard. They were exposed to cold and hunger, and were subjected to incessant pressure to do their best in every way: to develop skills and dexterity, a capacity to endure, courage, and power of judgment. They were severely punished if they fell short of the required standard or committed any error.[34] This severity was maintained long after the greatness of Sparta had waned. Plutarch, living several centuries later (first to second century A.D.), relates how he himself saw Spartan boys expire under the lash at the altar of Artemis Orthia. He cites this[35] as an argument in support of the reliability of old accounts of Spartan hardiness, such as that of Xenophon.[36]

The ideal of *aretē* was constantly impressed upon the young, through the heavy demands made on them, by the force of example, and by poetry. The poems of Tyrtaeus from the seventh century B.C. remained an important influence in Spartan up-bringing, known to everybody, recited at festivals and sung by the warriors as they walked forth on to the field of battle, 'Abide then, O young men, shoulder to shoulder and fight; begin not foul flight nor yet be afraid, but make the heart in your breasts both great and stout, and never shrink when you fight the foe ... So let each man bite his lip with his teeth and abide firm-set astride upon the ground.'[37] Numerous reliable sources testify that this ideal was carried through into real life. Throughout three centuries — from 669 B.C., when she was beaten by King Pheido of Argos, until 371, when she succumbed to the Thebans at Leuctra — Sparta lost only one battle, at Tegea in Arcadia in 560 B.C.* Otherwise nobody proved able to beat a Spartan corps unless it was grossly outnumbered, or where circumvention was possible, as for instance at Thermopylae in 480 or in Attica in 425 B.C. In one of Greece's most fateful hours, in 479 B.C., the year after the destruction of the fleet of Xerxes at Salamis, his

---

* On the other hand, Tegea was a particularly painful experience: a Spartan corps invaded Tegeate territory to make the Tegeates their bondsmen or helots, carrying with it fetters for the job. It was defeated, and the Spartans had to work the fields they had come to conquer, bound in their own chains (W. G. Forrest, *A History of Sparta* (London, 1968), p. 73).

immense army stood facing the united Greek forces, much inferior in numbers, at Plataeae in Boeotia. At first the major part of the Greeks were thrown into confusion by the Persians and took flight; only the steadfastness of the heavily armed Spartan infantry, the Hoplites, made it possible for the rest of the Greeks to rally and carry through the counterattack by which the battle was won.*

Paiderasty formed an integral part of Dorian upbringing — which by its lofty ideals, immense demands and merciless severity reminds us of that of the North American Plains Indians and of the Japanese before the last war. Plutarch tells that when Spartan boys were twelve years old, 'then those who are the lovers of noble young boys, would seek their company'.[38] From that point, the lovers of the boys — *erastai* — were held responsible for their conduct and development and shared their honour as well as their dishonour. For instance, a certain lover was fined by the authorities because a boy who was his *erōmenos* cried out aloud during a fight.[39] The status of the *erastēs* was such that he had the right to appear on an equal footing with the boy's father and older brothers, and to defend the boy's interests before the assembly at the *agorá* (the town market-place).[40] Xenophon, who lived around 400 B.C., while Sparta was still in possession of its full power, was an Athenian nobleman. As a friend of the Spartan King Agesilaus he spent much of his life in the Peloponnese, and he knew Sparta well. He wrote about the Spartan constitution and stresses the Spartan view of the importance of paiderasty in the system of upbringing, 'I think I must say something about the love of boys (*paidikōn erōtōn*), because it too is related to upbringing'. He then says that Lycurgus, the legendary giver of Sparta's laws, considered it valuable for men of quality to seek the

---

* The unshakeability of Sparta's reputation is testified to by the general reaction in Greece to the fatal defeat at Leuctra. Forrest writes, 'It is hard to say who was most surprised, Sparta, the rest of Greece, or the Thebans themselves . . . incredulously the Athenians sent away the Boeotian herald who came to announce the victory . . .'(ibid. p. 130).

friendship of boys for whom they felt admiration, and whose development they would endeavour to further. This Lycurgus encouraged, regarding it as the best kind of upbringing.[41]

How rooted paiderasty was in the Dorian culture is demonstrated in Crete by the ritual manner in which such relationships were entered into. Ephorus was a historian who wrote in the fourth century B.C. while the Dorian culture was still alive; the information he gave is quoted by Strabo, a geographer living at the time of Christ. Ephorus tells us that the formalities in arranging a paiderastic relationship were like those in an actual marriage by capture.[42] When a Cretan nobleman felt that he wanted a certain boy to educate as his *erōmenos*, he would let it be known to the boy's family three or four days in advance that on such-and-such a day, in such-and-such a place, he intended to capture the boy. If the family considered him a worthy suitor, satisfactory in regard to his nobility and *aretē* — equal or superior to the boy in these respects — the capture was permitted to take place; to satisfy decorum a sham resistance was put up for a short time, after which the boy was left to the suitor. First he would take the boy to his *andreion* — the mess-hall where he had meals — and then to his estate in the country, where for two months or so the boy would live with him as his *erōmenos*. At the end of this period the boy returned to his family, bringing with him rich gifts; a suit of armour, an ox, a drinking cup, and other things of value. After the home-coming the ox was sacrificed to Zeus, and a feast was given. This constituted the beginning of the *erastēs-erōmenos* relationship. However, it seems that only boys of particular distinction and outstanding character were introduced to paiderasty in this stately manner. The gifts were so expensive that the man's friends had to contribute towards them. Thus it bestowed on a boy a particular honour to be captured in this way, and thereafter he was given the title *klēnós*, meaning 'famous', a title he retained in adulthood. Such boys were better dressed than the others and were given the best seats at dances and races. The costly custom of giving the boy a suit of armour also existed in Thebes.[43]

Correspondingly, it was shameful for a boy of respectable lineage if no good man came forward wanting him for his *erōmenos*. This would be an indication of shortcomings in his character[44] — it would mean that he was not sufficiently *agathós*: good, proper, possessing the right qualities of personality. Similarly, if a man had made it known that he wanted to capture a boy, it was dishonourable for him to be found unworthy by the relatives of the boy. A man who offered himself, but was rejected, had been put to shame; his nobility and *aretē* had been slighted. This is the explanation, Bethe says, of the sad fate of a boy in Corinth. His relatives refused to give him into the custody of Archias of the Heraclides and offered serious resistance to the attempted capture. Both parties had their hands on the boy, and they pulled so hard that he was torn to pieces.[45] Bethe says that the boy lost his life not through Archias's disappointed erotic passion, but through his defence of his honour. The case is not unique.[46] In Sparta the Ephors punished a man who, in his nobleness and *aretē*, was suitable as a tutor, but who did not want the trouble and responsibility involved in a paiderastic relationship.[47] And a boy was punished if he preferred a rich but baser man to a poor and noble one.[48]

So these love relationships were not private erotic enterprises. They took place openly before the eyes of the public, were regarded as of great importance by the state, and were supervised by its responsible authorities.

Against the background of our customary view of pederasty, as reflected in our laws, all this seems quite inconceivable. It is hard for us to imagine how a Dorian Hellene could possibly regard a relationship between a man and a boy as ethically serious, and valuable in the upbringing of the young; as offering an incentive to the man to be an example to the youth and involving the boy in a duty to develop according to this example. And yet this

Dorian attitude is described so frequently, and in such detail, that we cannot doubt its existence and importance. In the *Symposium* of Plato Phaedrus says, 'I for my part am at a loss to say what greater blessing a man can have in earliest youth than an honourable lover, or a lover than an honourable favourite.' This is the way to learn what is most important in life, namely, 'the shame that we feel for shameful things, and ambition for what is noble'.

Phaedrus continues:

Without these feelings it is impossible for city or person to perform any high and noble deeds. Let me then say that a man in love, should he be detected in some shameful act or in a cowardly submission to shameful treatment at another's hands, would not feel half so much distress at anyone observing it, whether father or comrade or anyone in the world, as when his favourite did; and in the selfsame way we see how the beloved is especially ashamed before his lover when he is observed to be about some shameful business. So that if we could somewise contrive to have a city or an army composed of lovers and their favourites, they could not be better citizens of their country than by thus refraining from all that is base in a mutual rivalry for honour; and such men as these, when fighting side by side, one might almost consider able to make even a little band victorious over all the world. For a man in love would surely choose to have all the rest of the host rather than his favourite see him forsaking his station or flinging away his arms; sooner than this, he would prefer to die many deaths: while, as for leaving his favourite in the lurch, or not succouring him in his peril, no man is such a craven that Love's own influence cannot inspire him with a valour that makes him equal to the bravest born.[49]

This is the background against which we must understand the young Dorian warrior who, tripping and falling on his face during the battle, cried out to his adversary to withhold the thrust till he had turned and exposed his breast. He did not want his *erōmenos* to find him with the death wound in his back, and thereby be led to believe that he had been killed fleeing before the enemy.[50] The same is told of a Cretan by Aelianus.[51] The eagerness to show oneself an example to the young is demonstrated in the story of the Thessalian Cleomachus, whom the citizens of Chalchis of Eoboea called in to help against the cavalry of the enemy. Cleomachus asked his *erōmenos* to witness the battle. The young man kissed him and put on his helmet for him; then Cleomachus broke forcefully through the ranks of the enemy, conquered, and fell. Thereafter the grave of Cleomachus was honoured by the citizens of Chalchis, and the introduction of paiderasty there was attributed to him.[52]

Fighting corps composed of pairs of lovers as proposed by Phaedrus and mentioned by Xenophon in his *Symposium*,[53] did in fact exist. The Sacred Band of Thebes, as it was called, was the backbone of the Theban army that conquered the Spartans of Leuctra in 371 B.C. under the leadership of Pelopidas and Epameinondas,* and again at Mantineia in 362 B.C. under Epameinondas. The Sacred Band consisted of pairs of lovers fighting side by side. Epameinondas himself fell together with his *erōmenos* Caphisodorus. The Sacred Band remained unconquered until, in 338 B.C., it was overcome by Philip of Macedonia at Cheironeia, where all were killed and lay on the battlefield pair by pair.

In Crete, too, fighting together in pairs must have been customary, because the beloved youth was called *parastathéns*: he who stands by another's side.

Theognis, a Dorian nobleman from Megara—a city located between Attica, Boeotia, and Corinth—who lived in the sixth

---

* An entirely new and effective battle order, tried out for the first time by the Thebans, probably also contributed to the victory! However, the possible importance of one factor does not necessarily preclude the other. Morale and tactics may supplement each other.

century B.C., left a famous book addressed to his young friend
Cyrnus to whom he speaks as teacher, model, and lover. He
says to Cyrnus, 'I shall hand down to you the advice I received
from good men in my own childhood'.[54] As Jaeger[55] says, the
teaching of Theognis was not to impart his thinking as an individual but to express the traditional wisdom of his class. Its
didactic and erotic aspects were inseparable throughout. The eros
of Theognis served as the driving force in transferring his *aretē* to
Cyrnus.

The Dorian ideas on upbringing have been well summarized
by Bethe in the following passage:

The qualities of the man, his heroism, his *aretē*, are in some
way transmitted to the beloved boy through love. Therefore
it is society's view that skilful and competent men ought to
love boys; the state even exerts pressure on them to do so.
So the boys offer themselves to the heroes. In this way, the
erastēs and the *erōmenos* share fame and shame; and thus the
erastēs is made responsible for the cowardice of his beloved.
Therefore he is as legitimate a guardian of the boy as the
boy's next of kin. Thus it is that the man takes into consideration first of all the disposition of the boy he chooses; and
the *aretē* of the man is examined even more carefully to
know whether it is worthy of being transferred to the boy.
This is why the boy was shamed who did not find a lover,
and why, on the other hand, it was an honour for a boy to
have found an honourable lover and be ceremoniously
united with him, an honour which in Crete was celebrated
in public by the family. For this reason the honourable title,
klēnoi, was given to the boys who partook of a man's love.
This explains their distinguished dress and the respect paid to
them on public occasions, not just once but in perpetuity, the
reason being that through love these boys had become the
possessors of *aretē* to which these marks of distinction were

due. Plato shows clearly the deep-seatedness of the belief in the ennobling of boys through love and how widespread it was. In the *Symposium* Aristophanes is made to say, 'Only those play their role in the state who in their boyhood experienced a man's love'.[56]

Basic to the understanding of the nature, meaning, and importance of paiderasty is the following:

Firstly, the age difference between an *erastēs* and his *erómenos* was always considerable. The *erastēs* was a grown man, the *erómenos* still an immature boy or youth. As we have seen, this is shown clearly on the vase painting on Fig. 1 and on numerous other *kalós* vases. The younger of the pair is always a boyish figure; he is beardless, and is never depicted phallicly. Whenever his genital is drawn clearly, as on many fifth- and fourth-century red-figure vases, it is shown to be that of a pre-pubertal boy and is never erect. From many sources it emerges that the role of the youth as an *erómenos* came to an end when he reached the close of adolescence, as signified by the first growth of beard. Pindar's *Ode* (quoted on p. 28) describes the erotic relationship of Poseidon to Pelops as ending when the first beard darkened the cheeks of Pelops, and Theognis tells Cyrnus, 'As long as your cheek is smooth I shall not cease courting you'.*[57] Among the Ionians, erotic relationships are known to have existed between grown men, but then the difference of age was also considerable, as in the case of the philosophers Parmenides and Zenon,[58] or Socrates and Alcibiades.[59]

Secondly, as has been demonstrated, an ethical basis was essential for the Dorian relationship. Ephorus says of the Cretans, 'It is not the boy who is unusually handsome whom they regard as a worthy object of love, it is the boy who is eminent in respect to manliness and decency'.[60] This is reflected in the very

---

* In some cases erotic relations are bound to have continued beyond adolescence, cf. for example the Sacred Band of Thebes.

word used about the boy by the Dorians — in the Thera inscriptions, for instance, *agathós* or its superlative, *áristos* — a word expressing the proper aristocratic qualities of a man — is the adjective derived from the noun *aretē*. In Athens, however, the Ionians said of a boy that he was *kalós*, the predominant meaning being handsome, attractive.

Thirdly, the homosexuality of the paiderastic relationship had nothing to do with effeminacy. On the contrary, among the Dorians the obvious aim of education was manliness in its most pronounced forms. Refinement in the manner of dressing and in regard to food, houses, furniture or other circumstances of daily life was looked upon with contempt. Contemporary as well as later sources agree in stressing that it was among the warlike Dorians in particular that paiderasty flourished.[61]

Fourthly, Dorian paiderasty was something entirely different from homosexuality in the usual sense in which we use the term, as inversion (see the definition p. 17). We have repeatedly pointed out that ordinary men regularly cultivated paiderasty and active heterosexuality at the same time. Men who stuck exclusively to boys and who did not marry were punished, scorned, and ridiculed by the Spartan authorities, and treated disrespectfully by the young men. Plutarch says that men in Sparta remaining bachelors beyond the ordinary age for marriage were forbidden to be present when the young men and girls were exercising. In addition, once a year they had to walk naked around the market-place, in a group, singing a song in scorn of their unmarried state. In the same context Plutarch tells us about a young man who refused to give up his seat to the older, unmarried Dercyllidas with the derisory remark that he, Dercyllidas, would never have sons who in turn could offer their seats to him, the young man, when he grew old. This, Dercyllidas had to put up with, eminent general though he was.[62]

So neither the older nor the younger man was homosexually

inverse in our sense. On the contrary, the Spartans discriminated against men who were inverse.

Finally it is vital to rid oneself of the prejudice, repeated over and over with astonishing monotony in philological, historical, and psychiatric literature, that men in Hellas loved each other because women were not worthy of their interest; because women were ignorant and lacking in culture, inhibited by the suppressed condition in which they were kept by their menfolk, held in seclusion in their homes without political influence and deprived of the slightest possibility of spiritual and intellectual development. The belief is that they were thus dulled by bondage to domestic toil, nowadays so much despised.

This view is quite untenable. In the first place, it is not through intellectual achievement or by their accomplishments in public life that women exert erotic attraction on men. Regardless of women's importance in the intellectual and political life of our time, it is (as it is also in the case of those who distinguish themselves in these fields) by their other qualities that they make men reach out for them — qualities which have nothing to do with ability in speculation and discourse. Such simple reasoning exposes the fallacy of the idea that boredom in the spiritual realm made the Hellenes reject the eroticism of their women for that found among boys and young men.

This apart, the position of women in the Dorian states was one of particular freedom and equality with men. The girls of Sparta were trained like the young men in bodily exercises — even in throwing the spear and discus — and in music and dancing. They very often attended games and festivals with the boys and youths.[63] So they had every opportunity of cultivating common interests, which we conceive to be the soundest basis for a happy married life. In the daily life of Sparta, women were highly influential as administrators of the home and of the family estates while the men were at war — which was often, and for long periods of time. The freedom and independence of the Dorian

woman was generally recognized in contemporary Greece. To
regard her as suppressed and inferior is as mistaken as it would be
to suppose the same of Norse women, who did not attend political
assemblies with the men either.

The usual cliches about suppressed women in a society dominated by males do not pertain even to the Athenian woman, who
was more confined to her home and not trained in bodily exercises. In his fine book *The Greeks*, Kitto makes this the subject of
a penetrating investigation, beginning:

> Most men are interested in women, and most women in
> themselves. Let us therefore consider the position of women
> in Athens. It is the accepted view, challenged so far as I know
> by nobody except A. W. Gomme, that the Athenian
> woman lived in an almost Oriental seclusion, regarded with
> indifference, even contempt. The evidence is partly the
> direct evidence of literature, partly the inferior legal status
> of women.

Kitto's argument, which he fully substantiates, shows how
faulty this conception is: it is not supported by the available
material; is contradicted by literary sources (including those used
in its support—which, seen in context, must be understood quite
differently); contradicted, too, by the testimony of vase paintings
and sculptured tombstones depicting the relationship between
husband and wife; and contradicted further by the fact that
Athenian women attended the public performances of the great
tragedies—you do not comprehend Aeschylus if you are narrow-
minded and ignorant! The prejudice regarding the relationship of
men to women in Hellas is based only on misinterpretation and
on naïve, biased conclusions projected backward from modern
life in the big cities of northern Europe and America. I would
recommend anyone interested in the subject to read these sixteen
pages in Kitto's book—his treatment of the subject, incidentally,
is not concerned with paiderasty, a phenomenon of such scant

interest to him that he devotes a mere seven lines to it out of a total of 250 pages.*[64]

One further detail: in his laws Solon decrees that the legal validity of an obligation may be annulled if a man enters into it under pressure from his wife. Solon places this on an equal footing with obligations entered into under coercion.[65] In view of this, it is hardly conceivable that the Athenians did not ascribe importance and influence to their wives in the early sixth century B.C., when Solon also wrote his lines in praise of paiderasty.

In spite of the distance in time between us and the people we have been dealing with, and although the form and style of their lives differed from ours, they were basically similar to us. In the next chapter we will make a jump into our own time to see how homosexual elements manifest themselves in men who relate normally to women in our society. Experience from the present may throw light on the life of the ancients, just as reflections from that time, long ago, may well enrich our own knowledge of ourselves.

NOTES

1. Hiller von Gärtringen, *Thera* (1896–1901), III, p. 67 ff., and *Inscriptiones Graecae* XII, 3, 537.
2. Plutarch, The Dialogue on Love, *Moralia* 751 B and *The Life of Solon* I, 3.
3. Plutarch, *The Life of Solon* I, 3.
4. Plutarch, The Dialogue on Love, *Moralia* 751 C.
5. Op. cit. 751 E.

* Apart from the slave woman who might be the concubine of the master of the household, there existed in Athens a comprehensive system of organized prostitution, fully recognized and accepted, consisting of: *Hetaerae* who were respected women with an education in art and literature, as in the case of the *Aspasia* of Pericles, corresponding to the Japanese Geishas; the *Auletrides*, flute players, who also mastered dancing and acrobatics, present in Plato's *Symposium* as well as Xenophon's; *Dicteriades*, the common street prostitutes, many of whom did not even have a room of their own; they found shelter with their customers in the great temple of Aphrodite Pandemus. How would all these prostitutes have made a living if Athenian men were uninterested in women?

6. J. M. Edmonds, *Elegy and Iambus* I, 27.

7. Ibid.

8. Op. cit. I, lines 1253–6.

9. Op. cit. I, lines 1335–6.

10. Xenophon, *Anabasis* IV, 1, 14.

11. Op. cit. II, 6, 6.

12. Xenophon, *The Constitution of Sparta* II, 12—see also Xenophon, *Symposium* VIII, 34.

13. Pindar, *Olympia* I (there is a good English translation by Owen Lattimore, *The Odes of Pindar* [Chicago, 1955]).

14. Pindar fragment of 10 lines, preserved by Athenaeus, XIII, 601 d–e.

15. E. Bethe, *Thebanische Heldenlieder* (Leipzig, 1891), where the sources are given.

16. Plutarch, The Dialogue on Love, *Moralia* 750 B.

17. Plato, *The Laws* 836 C.

18. Hans Licht, *Sittengeschichte Griechenlands* (Stuttgart, 1965), p. 108.

19. Op. cit., p. 93.

20. Plutarch, The Dialogue on Love, *Moralia* 754 E and *Diodorus* IV, 31, 1.

21. Plutarch, The Dialogue on Love, *Moralia* 761 E.

22. Pauly-Wissowa, *Realencyclopädie*, s.v. *Polymnos*, p. 1773.

23. A. Nauck, *Tragicorum Graecorum Fragmenta*, second edition (Leipzig, 1889), 135.

24. Plutarch, The Dialogue on Love, *Moralia* 751 C.

25. Quoted from Hans Licht, op. cit.

26. Athenaeus, book XIII, 601 a.

27. E. Bethe, *Die Dorische Knabenliebe, ihre Ethik und ihre Idee* (Rheinisches Museum für Philologie, Neue Folge, 1907).

28. Xenophon, *Hiero* I, 31 ff.

29. Werner Jaeger, *Paideia*, I (Oxford, 1946), p. 3 ff.

30. Vilhelm Grønbech, *Hellas* I (Copenhagen, 1961), p. 19 f.

31. Homer, *The Iliad* 15, 642.

32. Pindar, *Pythia* 20, 23.

33. Pindar, *Olympia* 7, 89.

34. Strabo, 10, 4, 20, and Plutarch, *The Life of Lycurgus* XII, 4 and XVII.

35. Plutarch, ibid. XVIII, 2.

36. Xenophon, *The Constitution of Sparta* II.

37. J. M. Edmonds, *Elegy and Iambus* I, *Tyrtaeus* 10.

38. Plutarch, *The Life of Lycurgus* XVII, 1.

39. Op. cit. XVIII, 7.

40. Op. cit. XXV, 1.

41. Xenophon, *The Constitution of Sparta* II, 12–13.

42. Strabo, 10, 4, 21.

43. Plutarch, The Dialogue on Love, *Moralia* 761 B.

44. Strabo, 10, 4, 21.

45. Plutarch, The Dialogue on Love, *Moralia* 772 F.

46. Op. cit. 773 F.

47. Aelianus, *Varia Historia* III, 10.

48. Ibid.

49. Plato, *Symposium* 178 C–D.

50. Plutarch, The Dialogue on Love, *Moralia* 761 C, and *The Life of Pelopidas* 18.

51. Aelianus, *Historia Animalium* IV, 1.

52. Plutarch, The Dialogue on Love, *Moralia* 760 E–F. (The story was first told by Aristotle.)

53. Xenophon, *Symposium* VIII, 32.

54. Theognis, book I, lines 27–8.

55. Werner Jaeger, op. cit., I, p. 194.

56. E. Bethe, *Die Dorische Knabenliebe*, p. 457.

57. Theognis book II, lines 1327–8, Edmonds, *Elegy and Iambus* I.

58. Plato, *Parmenides* 127.

59. Plato, *Symposium* 215 ff.

60. Strabo, 10, 4, 21.

61. Plato, *Symposium* 182 A, and Plutarch, The Dialogue on Love, *Moralia* 761 D.

62. Plutarch, *The Life of Lycurgus* XV, 1–3.

63. Op. cit. XIV, 2–4.

64. H. D. F. Kitto, *The Greeks* (Chicago, 1964), p. 219–36.

65. Plutarch, *The Life of Solon* XXI, 4.

2

Men and Boys in the Present Day

For quite some time it has been known that homosexual feelings and acts occur among men far more frequently than most people imagine. We know this from patients, nervous but otherwise normal — particularly in their heterosexual attitudes — who tell us about themselves and the people around them. We have also received such information from doctors and psychologists, undergoing psychoanalysis for training purposes, who are not patients in the strict sense. Finally we know of it from a number of ordinary, normal people, belonging to no particular category, who just go through life with their eyes and ears open, and who register and remember their own experiences and those of others.

Nevertheless, this relatively common knowledge has been kept hidden, as a kind of public secret — under what Williamson[1] calls 'the conspiracy of silence' — as something only openly discussed in certain professional circles, among doctors or police experts, for instance. This was seen in the sensation — the actual disturbance — caused by the Kinsey report. Even with the crude and superficial methods of investigation which Kinsey used, it was established beyond doubt that on the average two out of every five men had bodily sexual contact, including orgasm, with another man at some time between sixteen years and old age.[2] Kinsey's figures were based on the face-to-face questioning of several thousand American men. The incidence of homosexual acts varies according to time and place. If a similar investigation were conducted among the Mohammedans of North Africa or in Turkey today, far more, if not all, men would confirm the frequent occurrence of homosexual episodes in their lives, not only before the age of thirty when the incidence is high, but also episodically or periodically in later life. Most likely these people would wonder why anybody should want to waste his time going around asking about things everybody already knew.

The situation is quite different in Denmark, where Erling Jacobsen[3] and Preben Hertoft[4] received affirmative answers from a much smaller percentage than Kinsey—less than ten per cent. The groups questioned by these research workers were small compared to Kinsey's. Both Jacobsen and Hertoft doubt the honesty of the replies, rightly in my opinion, although we have no way of knowing whether the incidence differs in Denmark and the U.S. However, if we broaden our field of interest to include the existence of conscious homosexual impulses, whether carried out in action or controlled, we have to add considerably to the figures given for manifest acts. This is particularly the case in youths between sixteen and twenty. If, furthermore, without resorting to subtle interpretation, we include all the men who have homosexual dreams, we reach numbers which show, not surprisingly of course, that a homosexual radical is present in all men today, just as it was in the time of the Greeks.

Whether or not we find this radical expressed in the actions of a grown man proves nothing in regard to his inherent propensities. Abstention is merely a measure of his will and ability to adjust to the demands of our civilization. Indeed, in obedience to our norms most grown men not only abstain from homosexual activity, but are not even conscious of any such inclination. If they had experiences of this kind in boyhood or youth, as temptations or as desires carried out in action, they have forgotten them. If they do have some such memory, it appears to them as lacking in significance, perhaps a little shameful, but to be recalled without erotic emotion.

The adjective 'unnatural' applied to homosexual phenomena is devoid of meaning. Homosexuality may be called 'uncultural' when it manifests itself against the rules of a culture, as for instance the Christian and Jewish ones.

So among men beyond the age of twenty-five who are normal or who merely have neurotic potency-disturbances, manifest homosexuality is rare in ordinary daily life. However, it does occasionally occur, and under certain circumstances it is not unusual. Kinsey says:

> ... in certain of the most remote rural areas there is considerable homosexual activity among lumbermen, cattlemen, prospectors, miners, hunters, and others engaged in out-of-door occupations. The homosexual activity rarely conflicts with their heterosexual relations, and is quite without the argot, physical manifestations, and other affectations so often found in urban groups. There is a minimum of personal disturbance or social conflict over such activity. It is the type of homosexual experience which the explorer and pioneer may have had in their histories.[5]

It must increase our understanding of the subject to compare with Dorian paiderasty what we know from our own civilization about grown men and boys before, during and in the years after puberty. A striking difference is immediately apparent. Among the Dorians it was the best men who cultivated paiderasty as something worthy of praise, as an obligation to the state, and men were punished if they did not meet this obligation. In our society, on the other hand, it is only a subgroup of the inverse homosexuals who have relationships with boys. They try to hide it as best they can, and they are condemned and punished if they are detected. Probably they correspond to the bachelors who were treated scornfully in Sparta. They differ from the average man in our society in their inability to adjust themselves heterosexually, in spite of the danger of punishment and social ruin; as a rule they are partially or totally impotent with women. So the grown man in a paiderastic relationship in our civilization is no counterpart to the Dorian *erastēs*. His problems are of a special nature, outside the context of the subject we are concerned with.

This is not so with boys, however. Any boy, no matter how normal and well adjusted in his family and in society, may be found to be engaged in a paiderastic relationship, but if so it is not indicative of future abnormalities in his heterosexual development.

To a considerable extent this phenomenon has also been the subject of 'the conspiracy of silence'. It is not well known to the public. On the contrary, in many quarters there is a good deal of worry and fuss when a boy is found to be involved in sexual relations with one of his own sex. However, professional people in certain categories—members of the police for instance—know how readily boys respond homosexually. A former director of the Copenhagen police force wrote that it was 'quite exceptional for boys to withstand energetic seduction on the part of a grown man'—a statement endorsed by Police Inspector Jens Jersild.[6] To this should be added that young boys are easily seduced by older boys, just as they seduce each other. Furthermore it is by no means rare for the boy to be the seducer of the older youth or man. Although reasoning is not one of the outstanding qualities of the Kinsey Report, a good point is made in this connection. After discussing the younger boy's admiration for masculine prowess and his desire to emulate older boys, the Report continues, 'The anatomy and functional capacities of male genitalia interest the younger boy to a degree that is not appreciated by older males who have become heterosexually conditioned and who are continuously on the defensive against reactions which might be interpreted as homosexual.'[7] This may be understood to be closely connected with the powerful tendency of the normal boy to select models to admire and imitate from among older boys and grown men. This tendency is an indispensable factor in the development of boys and aids them in their endeavour to acquire the desirable qualities of their elders through identifying with them. Strong feelings of attachment and love form part of these relationships and further the development of the boys. The prototype is the boy's relationship with his father. As Fenichel puts it, 'Every boy loves his father as a model whom he would like to resemble; he feels himself the "pupil" who, by temporary passivity, can achieve the ability to be active later on. This type of love could be called the apprentice love.'[8] What Fenichel refers to by the word 'passivity' is the submission of the boy in this situation. Although a stealthy interest in the genital of the father is the rule with small boys, it is suppressed as they grow older, and in boys in pre-puberty and later, conscious interest is directed towards the genitals of other men and youths.

A contemporary Danish writer, Klaus Rifbjerg, has painted a vivid and true picture of these relationships in a couple of his stories. In *The Public Baths* he describes a pre-pubertal boy's intense preoccupation with the difference between his own inconspicuous genital — 'ours are mostly alike and of the same colour as the rest of the body ... ' — and the big organs of the grown men, so different in different men, and so interesting in their detail that as you looked at them you might begin to feel warm, and your penis embarrassingly start to swell. A boy's voice runs through the whole story telling of something important which could never be told to the grown-ups.

In another story, *Naughty Jensen*, Rifbjerg describes a love-relationship, broad and deep in meaning, existing between a band of boys and a grown man, a small shopkeeper, living on the outskirts of Copenhagen: 'We liked Jensen, though we took advantage of him — or he of us, as the police or child-welfare authorities would probably have said; but the fact simply was that we could not do without him.' 'You felt as though you were taking an oath,' the boy goes on to explain, when you were standing with your hand on Jensen's erect penis, experiencing the strength of it; then you became strongly aware of the world in all its detail and at the same time as a unified whole. In other words, Rifbjerg describes how Jensen's penis turned into a phallus for the boys, filled with meaning and pointing far beyond itself and the present situation; it 'pointed out a direction'. When one of the boys denounces Jensen the others take a cruel revenge on him.*

Of course there are numerous cases where a boy's admiration for an older hero is mixed with strong erotic feelings, without there being any bodily involvement.

In order to understand the boy's position in a homosexual relationship, it is important to be aware that the pre-pubertal boy, his genitals not yet developed from the infantile state, may experience strong sensual tension towards an older boy or a man and be attracted by their mature genitals without feeling any genital sensations to speak of and also without wanting to be stimulated genitally himself. His pleasurable experience may be a more generalized one, physically and emotionally, while his interest is predominantly directed towards seeing and touching the genitals of his older partner and feeling a general bodily contact with him.† It is important to appreciate this in order to understand the development of the male in general, and, more particularly, the nature and meaning of Dorian paiderasty, which began in pre-puberty.

It is evident, of course, that in and after puberty boys may experience genital pleasure and satisfaction. To understand how a normal boy develops, it is necessary to recognize the importance of this homosexual element, and to acknowledge how indispensable it is for his growth from childhood to maturity. There is no doubt that most boys experience pressure from their sexual drive,

---

* Both tales are from a collection, *And other stories*, which unfortunately is not available in translation. Danish, *Og andre historier* (Copenhagen, 1964).

† There are boys who have not only erection, but orgasm too — without the emission of semen, of course — before puberty, even in their first years of life. However, this is mostly a masturbatory phenomenon and rarely occurs in the present context.

with a consequent receptivity to sensual stimulation and the need
for sexual discharge—this is unequivocally expressed by the frequent and regular masturbatory activity of practically all boys in
puberty and adolescence. Nevertheless, it is just as undeniable that
the sexual element does much more for the boy than serve his erotic pleasure and gratification. One may generalize and say that the
erect genital and its function have a symbolism for males in
general and boys in particular.

A symbol is an image, usually visual, a picture which comes to
the mind in thought, fantasy, or dream and which has, underlying it, a multiplicity of meanings and feelings.* By the symbolic
term phallus, we express the idea that beyond the practical
function of the genital in its fully erect shape as a means of procreation and pleasure, it is a pictorial representation of the essence
of manliness, a representation of the synthesis of every imaginable
aspect of proper manhood. Thus for the boy, the phallus repre-
sents the grown man's greatness, strength, independence, courage, wisdom, knowledge, mastery of other men and possession
of desirable women, potency—and everything else a boy may
look up to in men and desire for himself. Many of the meanings
and feelings concentrated in the phallus are remote from current
ideas of sex, and often they are mutually contradictory, as for
example the ability to dominate and to give oneself. Most of them
are implicit, rarely are they immediately grasped, instantly ex-
pressible in words. They exist in action, attitude and feeling. It is
the important function of symbols in our mental life to be unitary,
nonverbal expressions of the manifold and the self-contradictory
—of all that is meaningful and important in human life, but for
which it is difficult or impossible to find complete, unequivocal
expression in words. In a symbol expression is possible, the
role of the symbol being precisely that of expressing the mani-

---

* An allegory is also a pictorial representation, but one chosen deliberately to stand for
a predetermined meaning. The same applies to semiotic signs — x and y in mathematics
for instance — which however are not pictorial, but abstract.

fold in the one—and without the manifold being lost in the oneness.

For the boy, the symbolic meaning of the phallus is closely
allied to physical drives, and this is the reason why he is so fasci-
nated by the mature male genital. Because of the boy's burning
wish to develop into manhood in the image of the men and
youths he admires, it is easy for the older male to get the boy to
worship his genital and treat it to his satisfaction. The boy may
possibly take the initiative himself to establish a contact of this
kind.

The importance of the phallic symbol for the grown man appears in many connections, for instance in a marked form in the
general loss of self-esteem felt by a man if his sexual potency fails.
His painful feeling that his abilities have been reduced over a wide
range, far beyond that of sex, is one of the signs that the genital
function stands for much more and many other things than the
pleasures of Aphrodite.

The frequent anxiety dreams of five- to seven-year-old boys
that their penes have been harmed or destroyed, have the same
origin; 'My dickie was torn to pieces by a big dog', a boy reported after waking up with a cry. It is their whole feeling of manhood which is threatened; hence the intense anxiety. The fundamental difference between men and women emerges particularly
clearly on this point. A general loss of self-esteem affecting the
total personality is not seen in frigid women or in women who,
in spite of willingness, are hampered by deficiencies in their ability to respond sexually.

Thus men of all ages still worship the phallus, although we have
no institutionalized phallic cult such as exists among numerous
other peoples of the world or such as existed at other times, for
instance in old Scandinavia before it adopted Christianity or in
ancient Greece. The phallic cult among the Greeks will be described in the next chapter.

NOTES

1. Hugh Ross Williamson, *The Arrow and the Sword* (London, 1955), p. 79 ff.
2. A. C. Kinsey, W. S. Pomeroy and C. E. Martin, *Sexual Behaviour in the Human Male* (Philadelphia and London, 1948), p. 623 ff.
3. Erling Jacobsen, *Dissertation, Psykoneuroser* (Copenhagen, 1965).
4. Preben Hertoft, 'Investigation into the Sexual Behaviour of Young Men', *Danish Medical Bulletin*, vol. 16, Suppl. 1 (1969), pp. 64–5.
5. Kinsey et al., op. cit., p. 631.
6. J. Jersild, *Barnet og det homoseksuelle problem* (Copenhagen, 1957), p. 31 ff.
7. Kinsey et al., op. cit., p. 168.
8. O. Fenichel, *The Psycho-Analytic Theory of Neurosis* (New York, 1945), p. 334.

3

Phallic Worship in Ancient Greece

Phalli are found in Greece from every period back to the early Stone Age.[1] In archaic and classical times, phallic worship was a prominent feature of the religion of the Hellenes. At the temples and in front of the houses of Athens stood *hermas* like the one seen in Figure 4, on which the sculptor is working. The *herma* was a four-sided column with a man's head and a protruding phallus, but without arms and legs. So, approaching a house, the first thing one met at the front door was a phallus. (It is interesting to note that similar *hermae* exist today in parts of the world far from Greece, such as Timor, Celebes, Borneo and Nias. They are carved from wood and are erected at the door for protection of the house. Figure 27 shows a *herma* from Nias. Members of the household offered sacrifices to it regularly. It is evident that this kind of holy picture, the object of a cult, was bound to have had a symbolic meaning beyond the sphere of sexuality in the accepted, narrow sense of the word.* *Hermas* also stood at crossroads. The religious significance of the *herma* in the classical period stands out in Thucydides' report upon the reason why Alcibiades was exiled from Athens during the Peloponnesian war. One night in the spring of the year 415 B.C., the *hermas* of

---

* This is clearly expressed by Plutarch. The *hermas* of ancient times, he says, had the heads of old men and an erect genital, but no hands and feet. Plutarch explains that they have a phallus and no limbs because the bodily abilities of old men were unnecessary; only their brains had to be alive and fertile. (Plutarch, *Moralia* 797.) So the phallus is equivalent to brains.

the city were mutilated. Only one is said to have remained
unharmed. This was regarded as the gravest sacrilege and as an
evil omen for the impending expedition against Sicily. Rewards
were offered for information, and the security of the informants
guaranteed. It then occurred to the enemies of Alcibiades to
accuse him of being behind the misdeed; his groundless trial resulted, and he was forced to go into exile. Aristophanes alludes
to the same incident of the defacing of the *hermas*. In *Lysistrata*
the Spartan envoys arrive to negotiate with the Athenian Prytanis
for peace, and all appear with immense phalli (as a result of
the women withholding their favours for a prolonged period).
The chorus now advises the Spartans and the Prytanis to wrap
their cloaks about themselves 'in order that the *herma*-smashers
shall not lay eyes on you'. The *herma* reveals the importance of the
phallus in the domestic cult. The festivals of Dionysus, which were
kept in individual households, in villages, and by the state itself,
also offer proof of the religious significance of the phallic symbol.
Huge phalli were carried in procession at these festivals. In the
Acharnians Aristophanes pictures for us the procession at a private
festival in honour of Dionysus, celebrated by the good man
Dicaeopolis, his daughter, and his slave Xanthias. The occasion is
the peace concluded between Athens and Sparta. The wife of
Dicaeopolis is a spectator on the roof of the house. First Dicaeopolis invokes Dionysus:

> Lord Dionysus, grant me now
> To show the show and make the sacrifice
> As thou would'st have me, I and all my house;
> Then keep with joy the Rural Dionysia.

> (lines 247–50)

Thereupon he arranges the procession, and orders Xanthias to
hold the phallus pole erect. Then he sings the phallic hymn, beginning thus:

O Phales, comrade revel-roaming
Of Bacchus, wanderer of the gloaming,
Lover of wives and boys,
Here in my home I gladly greet ye.

(lines 263–6) *†

The sixth-century vase-painting illustrated in Figure 5 shows a phallus pole. Six men are carrying the base from which the phallus pole projects obliquely upwards, surrounded by the ivy vines of Dionysus.

The great Dionysia, in Athens for instance, were important occasions of state, celebrated with pomp, and they attracted spectators from far away. Huge phalli in great numbers were carried forth in the procession, and the participants had big artificial phalli strapped on to them. Members of the chorus of the comedies given during the festival at the theatre of Dionysus were equipped in the same way.

Because of the importance of the role of the phallus in the Dionysian festivals, a phallus would be sent to the festival of a new colony by the city from which the colony originated.[3]

Phallic images were also used as grave monuments, particularly to commemorate those who had covered the expenses of the theatrical performances.[4]

It has been shown that phallic worship and paiderasty have prominent places in the Greek pattern of life. They are interconnected in cult; Dionysus is called both *phalēs* and *paiderastēs*: *phalēs* is the name of the phallus personified, and *paiderastēs*, as we know, means a lover of boys. An interconnection between the two is also indicated by the fact that the Thera inscriptions, which speak of fulfilled paiderasty as a religious act, are found at

---

* The Loeb edition translation, with a slight change in line 265 to bring it closer to the Greek text.

† Regarding the striking similarity to the description of Norse phallic cult in the Edda's *Song of Vølse*, see p. 85.

the temple of Apollo Carneius. Carneius means 'the horned', and
the horned Apollo was a Dorian ram god; an archaic stele, dedi-
cated to Apollo Carneius, carries the horns of a ram.[5] Horned
gods are phallic gods everywhere: Baal (the bull of gold), the
Indian god from Mohenjo-Daro (Figure 6), the Greek Pan and the
masked dancer in the cave painting from Fourneau de Diable
(Figure 7), to mention only a few examples. In addition the image
of Apollo Carneius is found on a *herma*.[6]

The connection between phallic worship and Dorian paiderasty
contributes to an understanding of the latter. The paiderastic act
assumes epochal proportions in the life of the boy on account of
the symbolic character of the phallus. As Wilamowitz-Moellen-
dorf states, 'We must accept that for the Hellenes the phallus
symbolized the full force of manliness, not just procreative power.
This would apply to gods as well as to mortals.'[7] 'The full force
of manliness' is the *aretē* of the man. The phallus is the symbol of
aretē with all its complexities of meaning. Apollo's power of
manliness is concentrated in his phallus, and as Crimon, invoking
Apollo, celebrated the paiderastic act with the son of Bathycles,
he transferred his *aretē* to the boy through his phallus with the
help of the god.

It is worth noting that the Hellenes made a clear distinction
between phallus as a symbol and the anatomical organ, using a
different term for the latter. 'Phallus' was used only in a religious
context. Anatomically the genital is called by other names, *'peos'*
(tail), for instance.

Bethe has pointed out that it is the semen of the man, admini-
stered to the boy *per anum*, which is the carrier of his *aretē*.[8] Corresponding observations were made by the Finnish anthropologist
G. Landtmann when he lived among the Kiwai Papuans by the
Torres Strait during the years 1910–12. In certain villages at festivals celebrating the initiation of puberty, anal coitus was practised on the young to make them 'tall and strong'.[9] For the same
reason the chief Mainou would give the young warriors his urine

to drink to give them strength and fighting spirit, and they would be given also small pieces of the dried penis of a slain enemy to eat.[10] Modern religious historians speak of the transference of *mana*; it may be said of the Dorian that his *mana* was in his seed.

Anal coitus must also have had a central place in the Etruscan culture. Figure 8 shows a wall-painting from an Etruscan grave, sixth century B.C. — roughly contemporary with the vase-painting in Figure 1 and a hundred years later than the Thera inscriptions. A man is seen performing anal coitus on another man; the latter is without a phallic attribute, which seems to emphasize his submissive, receptive role.* What is found on the walls of graves must have some religious meaning.

Apollo Carneius being a Dorian god, it might be expected that the paiderastic act, carried out in public at the temple of Apollo, was in the first place an initiation rite shared by all Dorians. Certainly initiation in Sparta and on Thera must originally have taken place in the same way. We are safe in drawing this conclusion because Thera was colonized from Sparta in the eighth century B.C.,[11] and we know that religious customs and other important institutions were always taken from the mother city; thus the *Ephorate*† was taken to Thera from Sparta, and again from Thera to its colony Cyrene.[12] Correspondingly, the ritual paiderasty would have been brought to Thera by the Spartan colonizers.

In this context it cannot be emphasized too strongly how different we are from these people in our way of thinking and our ideas of reality. We speak of religious matters as something 'believed

* Of course I am aware that on Attic vases male skin is usually painted dark and female skin white. However, the lighter of the two figures in question is not white. It is conspicuously lighter than the other figure, the phallic one, which is black, but its colour is yellow and definitely contrasts with the *white* colour of the skin of a woman painted above another door a short distance to the left. The figure's light colour may simply denote his submissive role in the situation, perhaps his younger age. (Personal communication from Dr P. J. Riis of the University of Copenhagen.)

† The *Ephorate* was the ruling authority of Sparta, consisting of two *Ephors*, always chosen for a fixed period. The two hereditary kings had no authority in Sparta itself, only in the field in wartime.

in', as convictions which we may choose whether or not to adopt.
For example, there are many among us who do not 'believe in'
the Sacrament. They consider it an illusion that the ritual of Holy
Communion could exert a real influence on the fate of people
here or in the hereafter. The majority of those who attend the
Lord's Supper do so, supposedly, because it is part of their 'belief'
in Christ, a custom commemorating Him; what they feel as a
direct, subjective, here-and-now effect of drinking the wine and
eating the bread, is, I think, partly an emotional experience of
relief and freedom combined with the conviction that their sins
have been pardoned, and partly an alteration in their basic feeling
towards life as their belief and hope regarding the hereafter are
felt to be confirmed. Some people may experience other meanings
and dimensions in the receiving of the Sacrament; but whatever
it may mean for different people, there are undoubtedly only a
few to whom it is an unshakeable reality, in which they feel in the
very marrow of their bones that they have eaten the flesh of
Christ's body, and drunk His blood, and that by doing so they
have partaken of His qualities, with the consequence that their
characters and capabilities have been changed in His image.

With the Dorian and the Kiwai Papuan it was different. For
them the rite they performed was as real and had effects as tangible
as the felling of a tree or the killing of an enemy. We have no right
to call this illusion; it is rather we who have lost the ability to experience such reality. Nevertheless, it is a fact that a human being
may himself effect changes in his character, his qualities, and his
capabilities — within the limits of his constitution, of course. Such
endeavours are necessary to everyone's development and make
education possible and successful. The ability to change and develop in the image of the model — whether parent, friend or
teacher — is furthered not only by an admiring, respectful and
loving relationship with that person but also by the symbols expressing the qualities of the model and the aim of the education.
For the young Dorian the phallus of his tutor was a comprehen-

sive image of all the latter's qualities which he wanted to acquire. The firm conviction that it was in reality through the semen of the tutor that he received the *aretē* aided the boy in his efforts to change in the desired direction. So ritual paiderasty was a symbolic act with tangible effects on the development of the boy's personality.

Against this background the prohibition by Solon of paiderastic relationships between slaves and the sons of free men is understandable. The slave had only his own characteristics to transfer to a boy—qualities useful in the case of a slave, but not to one who was destined to become a lord. The slave had no *aretē* to hand over to the boy.

Later sources do not refer to the paiderastic act as part of a definite ritual at the initiation of a boy into manhood. The proclamations of the Thera inscriptions show that the rite referred to there was not a secret one. The conclusion to be drawn would seem to be that the physical act dropped out of the religious ceremony. But it survived in the general pattern of education—one of many examples of the way in which cultic features may become interwoven in the daily life of 'primitive' peoples. From the sources available there can be no doubt that paiderasty retained its physical aspect throughout archaic and classical times in Sparta, Crete, Boeotia and Elis. Even Plato says explicitly that paiderasty in Lacedaemon—Sparta—was carnal as it was in Crete.[13] Xenophon's protestations[14] that educational paiderasty in Sparta was not carnal but purely emotional, Lycurgus having forbidden bodily relations, must have been made in spite of his knowledge to the contrary in order to make the Spartans conform to the ideas of Socrates. This is Bethe's opinion as well; he calls Xenophon's statement a whitewashing operation. The distortion is the more striking since the majority of the ten thousand whom Xenophon led home through Asia Minor were Dorians, of whose paiderasty he speaks so simply and directly in the *Anabasis*, leaving no doubt about the carnal nature of these relationships (see p. 27).

E

Without giving proper credit to Bethe, Werner Jaeger* in his great work *Paideia*, published much later (1933), places paiderasty in its proper perspective in the Dorian system of education. Discussing the poems of Theognis he says:

> Cyrnus, the young man to whom the poems are addressed, was bound to Theognis by Eros. The poet obviously considers that bond to be the basis of the educational relationship; and it was meant to make man and boy a typical couple in the eyes of the class to which they both belonged. It is very significant that the first time we have an opportunity of studying Dorian aristocracy closely we should find that homosexual love is a ruling motive in their character ... It must be recognized that the love of a man for a youth or a boy was an essential part of the aristocratic society of early Greece, and was inextricably bound up with its moral and social ideals.

A little further on he says that paiderasty 'was involved in the highest conceptions of moral nobility and spiritual perfection' and again:

> Lovers who were bound by the male Eros were guarded by a deeper sense of honour from committing any base action, and were driven by a nobler impulse in attempting any honourable deed. The Spartan state deliberately made Eros a factor, and an important factor, in its educational system, its *agogē*. And the relation of the lover to his beloved had a sort of educational authority similar to that of the parent to the child; in fact, it was in many respects superior to parental authority at the age when youths began to ripen into manhood and to cast off the bonds of domestic authority and family tradition. It is impossible to doubt the numerous

---

* In the original German edition of 1933, Jaeger does not even refer to Bethe in the notes as he finally does in the English edition of 1946.

affirmations of the educational power of Eros, which reach their culmination in Plato's *Symposium*.[15]

In referring to Plato and his view of paiderasty, it is natural to describe the attitude of the Ionian Athenians towards the love of boys. Bethe and Jaeger both emphasize that as a consequence of Dorian influence paiderasty was held in high esteem by the Athenian nobility. However, it was never integrated within the culture of Athens as it was in the Dorian world. The love of boys remained in Athens a more personal, erotic, and aesthetic phenomenon. It has been stressed earlier that among the Dorians the typical predicate of the beloved boy was *agathós*, meaning 'good' in an ethical sense, while in Athens the word was *kalós*, 'beautiful', 'handsome', with an aesthetic-erotic bias.

Since it was not rooted in Athenian culture, a reaction against the sensual love of boys took place in Athens in the first half of the fourth century B.C., supported by the ageing Plato. Plato develops his point of view in the *Symposium*, in *Phaedrus*, and in the *Laws*. In the *Symposium* Socrates relates what he learned about love from the wise woman Diotima of Mantinea.[16] The ethical value of abstention from sensual love is stressed again in *Phaedrus* in the famous allegory of the black and the white horse.[17] Finally Plato formulates with extreme sharpness his rejection of bodily paiderasty in the *Laws*.[18]

Plato says that indeed you cannot help but love youths and that a strong element of sensual attraction is inherent in this love. However, this bodily appetite has to be conquered and renounced. The gain in tolerating frustration is twofold: firstly, the urge of the lover to find expression for his love may be directed solely towards the goal of cultivating the Good in the soul of the youth — without a thought of selfish satisfaction; secondly, by refraining from the experience of both sensual and emotional satisfaction of an erotic nature, the lover may reach a state of pure contemplation of the Good and the Beautiful, so that he may have the experience of seeing the Celestial Light—that experience which is described exhaustively in the Diotima speech in the same words and expressions as are employed everywhere and in every age to describe the mystical experience.

Nevertheless, Plato takes it for granted, throughout these splendid passages, that all men are subject to a strong urge to turn to youths and boys for sexual satisfaction. By stressing so strongly how much may be gained by suppressing this carnal desire, he is at the same time testifying to the great power of physical homosexual attraction. And when, probably as the first person in history, he calls physical homosexuality 'unnatural', it is still quite clear that he considers a disposition towards homosexuality to be universal. It is not this which is unnatural. It is only giving in to it which is regarded as being 'against nature'. Incidentally Plato, at least in his later years, was somewhat sceptical of all sexual activity, with women, too, unless it was in the service of procreation. It may be remembered that he became one of the fathers of gnosticism.

Of course, Platonic love, which cuts off sexual discharge with consequent far-reaching ethical and mystical effects, is an expression of the presence of the homosexual radical just as much as was the manifest bodily homosexuality of the Dorians.

I have dealt with the homosexuality of the Greeks as an institutionalized phenomenon, integrated in the culture in the service of education—*paideia*—for the furtherance of the supreme good, as the Dorians saw it. Homosexuality as a gratification of the senses and emotions—accepted or tolerated in so many parts of the world at all times—has taken a lesser place only because attention has been focused on its meaning and importance outside those areas of human existence customarily connected with sex. It is the symbolic function of homosexuality with which we are concerned—the means by which clear expression can be given to the most fundamental conditions of life and by which human personalities are moulded and changed in many important respects outside the sphere of sex.

I have left untouched a number of aspects of sexual symbolism, regardless of their importance. There is, for example, the phallus as a symbol of fertility or of creation in general. An Egyptian myth of the creation of the world relates how the god Atum, standing on the primordial mound in the primordial ocean, created the world by masturbation; from his phallus he first emitted Shu and Tephnet, air and moistness, brother and sister, and creation began. I have left aside material of a corresponding nature from Greek mythology since it, too, is outside the subject of this book; nor have I dealt with the male–female union in *Hieros Gamos* — the Sacred Marriage. Homosexuality in normal women has been excluded for the same reason and not because it did not exist or was unimportant — Plutarch tells us that the girls in Sparta had love relationships with noble women.[19] Likewise, I have omitted references to the cultic meaning and role of femininity *per se* as in the cult of Demeter, or to phallic worship by women as at the Haloa festival.

The reason why I have dealt predominantly with Dorian Greece is of course that strictly speaking it was there and only there that paiderasty was completely integrated as an institution in the culture. Having described it as a well-functioning institution I think I should emphasize that no idealization is involved on my part. Our civilization has commonly regarded the Dorians with antipathy as warlike, harsh, brutal and ruthless — and so indeed they were. In many important respects their ideal of manliness — their concept of *aretē* — meets with scant recognition from us. Few of us, if any, would be able to adjust to Sparta or manage even to survive (nor would we in Athens, as Kitto pointed out). I merely wish to show that in the Dorian culture as it was, given its idea of The Good Life, paiderasty served its purpose. Thus it became an institution.

Then too we should remember that admiration for the Spartans was almost unbounded in the rest of Greece — which we, in turn, admire. This is equally the case with the brutal Sparta of the fifth century, hostile as it was to beauty (see Xenophon and Plato). But Sparta had not always been what it became in the fifth century B.C. It is now reliably known that Sparta in the seventh century B.C. derived much joy from beauty and other kinds of pleasure, though the warlike ideal of manliness and paiderasty was already fully developed.

NOTES

1. Pauly-Wissowa, *Realencyclopädie*, s.v. *Phallos*, p. 1685.
2. Thucydides, book VI, 27–9.
3. W. Deubner, *Attische Feste* (Darmstadt, 1962).
4. M. P. Nilsson, *Geschichte der Griechischen Religion I* (Munich 1967), p. 292 f.
5. Ulrich von Wilamowitz-Moellendorff, *Der Glaube der Hellenen I* (1955), p. 88.   6. Ibid.   7. Op. cit., p. 157.
8. E. Bethe, *Die Dorische Knabenliebe*, p. 461 ff.
9. Gunnar Landtmann, *The Kiwai Papuans of British New Guinea* (London, 1927), p. 237.   10. Op. cit., p. 151.
11. W. G. Forrest, *A History of Sparta 955–192 B.C.* (London, 1968), p. 77.
12. Op. cit., p. 43.   13. Plato, *The Laws*, 836.
14. Xenophon, *The Constitution of Sparta* II, 12–13.
15. Werner Jaeger, *Paideia*, vol. I, p. 194 ff.
16. Plato, *Symposium*, from 201, especially 210–12.
17. Plato, *Phaedrus*, 250–6.   18. Plato, *The Laws*, 636 ff. and 836 ff.
19. Plutarch, *The Life of Lycurgus* XVIII, 9.

The numerous references in literature to Greek paiderasty are recorded in a long article by M. H. E. Meier in *Allgemeine Encyklopädie der Wissenschaften und Künste* (Leipzig, 1837), s. v. 'Päderastie'. It is an exhaustive piece of research into the literary sources, but contains no contribution to the understanding of the role of paiderasty in Greek culture.

The year after Bethe published his article an English treatise appeared — independently of Bethe's, in all probability. This was John Addington Symonds's *A Problem in Greek Ethics* (London, 1908). It shows insight in many respects, but is not comparable to Bethe's contribution.

4

Excursus on the Baboon

When a male baboon feels threatened by a stronger male he wards off the danger by assuming the attitude of a female in heat. He turns around with lifted tail and arched back, exposing his hind parts to the superior male. The latter then ceases to threaten and mounts the submissive one, imitating the act of mating.

This pattern, first described in 1932 by Zuckermann,[1] is typical not only of monkeys and apes, but of many other animals that live in troops, bands, packs or flocks structured by a fixed hierarchy.

An animal is said to present to another animal when it takes on the attitude of a female willing to be mounted. The female baboon presents to the male while she is in heat during the first half of her menstrual cycle. In this period the tissue of her hind parts is swollen, and the whole region, including the vaginal entrance, the clitoris, and the anus, is strongly coloured and protuberant. However, aside from procreation, presentation serves a variety of other socially important purposes, many of them completely asexual: it indicates subordination in the hierarchy; it is the sign that an animal is giving up his rivalry with another (for a female or for food, for instance); and it is a means of warding off the hostility of a stronger animal. This use of presentation as a signal of submission is found in particular among animals which are able to do each other serious harm, as is very much the case with baboons. The baboon is a strong animal with a very powerful bite, and its ability to grab, hold and tear adds to its fighting

power. Generally speaking, baboons are well equipped to muti-
late and to kill. They take flight before no predator but the lion.

Mounting and presentation are used as signals among baboons,
regardless of sex. For instance, a young male may present to an
older and stronger female, and she may mount him. Among the
females presentation and mounting are used in the same way.

Many animal species continually use sexual behaviour patterns
outside the specifically sexual sphere. Serving as they do to indicate differences of power, their role is decisive in the maintenance
of peace, security and stability in a troop of baboons. This is so
whether they are in captivity, under semi-natural conditions in a
game reserve, or in complete freedom. A troop of baboons—
numbering fifty to a hundred, occasionally more — is a firmly
organized entity, controlled by a small group of older dominating
males who stick together and support one another's authority.
They are at the top of the troop hierarchy, and all the other
baboons make way for them and present to them. At the same
time these dominating males constitute a centre of attraction for
the whole troop, which gravitates towards them. The newly born
and the very young together with their mothers keep close to the
older males. So do the females in heat which are totally mono-
polized by the dominating males. The female which is most in
heat at a given time keeps closest to the male to which she belongs.
She is automatically his favourite as long as her heat is at its
height. The subordinate males keep away from the females and
present to the dominating males if they fear they might have done
something to arouse displeasure.

If the attention of the lord of the family is otherwise occupied,
a female which is not the object of his courtship at the moment
may offer herself by presenting to one of the subordinate bachelors
who instantly mounts her. However, should the leader turn
around unexpectedly and discover the misdeed, she will take
flight, screaming and shaking her fists at the bachelor as if she had
been raped by him—like the wife of Potiphar!

Homosexual intercourse is seen frequently among members of both sexes. The bachelors often join a family with a dominating male and one or several females. The lord of the family may be found dallying or copulating with the bachelor in the presence of the females, which will take no notice. Zuckermann observed a friendship between an older grown male and a younger immature one, lasting for three years. The older baboon protected the younger in every way and often had intercourse with him. The relationship was terminated by the death of the younger partner during adolescence; a veritable *erastēs–erōmenos* relationship.

The subordinate bachelors seem to be inhibited and inactive sexually. This is probably because they are constantly subject to the threatening watchfulness of the lord. Their rut seems to be totally inhibited by their fear of him. This would coincide with the observations made on certain fish: when sexually aroused the male exhibits a brilliant red colour, but he loses his colour immediately a stronger male appears on the scene.

The tight and coherent organization of a group of baboons emerges particularly clearly when the troop is on the move. The younger ones form the periphery; they walk in front, at the sides and to the rear of the troop. In the centre are the oldest and strongest males, and with them are the mothers of the newborn together with the very young. In the event that the troop is threatened by a predator, the young on the periphery will raise an outcry, and the strong males will then quickly assemble in front of the enemy with the rest of the troop protected behind them.[2]

Rank, as a structuring principle, is essential to the social stability and the survival of a troop of baboons. Mounting and presentation are integrating factors in this social structure, being signals of dominance and submission.

A few years ago Wickler[3] described how baboons warned off members of other troops by sitting around the outside of the troop with their legs apart, exhibiting their penes (Figure 23).

The penis of the baboon may be retracted and invisible, or it may protrude, either pendent or in a state of partial or total erection. The redness of the naked penis is conspicuous against the dark fur. (Similar phenomena are observed in other monkeys, in the guenons, for instance, whose genitals are particularly conspicuous because the red colouring of the penis is set off by the blue of the scrotum.) Wickler stated in his paper that this straddled posture was asexual and was to be understood purely as an aggressively threatening gesture. He included drawings and photographs of different monkeys on guard with their legs apart and their penes protruding, pendent or erect. He also showed a picture of a small monkey spreading its legs and squirting urine from its erect penis towards its own image in the mirror—a monkey recognizes all the members of its own troop, of course, but not its own appearance; therefore it sees a stranger in the mirror.

A further interesting observation is that monkeys on the lower rungs of the ladder have penes of a smaller size and a paler colour than those at the top. This is said to be due to the inhibiting effect of the dominance of the superordinate males. It is the subordination which effects the development of the genitals, not the other way round. This interpretation fits in with the observation that the subordinate monkeys are sexually inactive and unable to assert themselves when being watched by the lord.

These facts clearly demonstrate that penis-exhibition can have a purely aggressive role; both the engorgement of the penis, causing enlargement and protrusion, and the contraction of the muscular tissue of the penis, causing the erection, may occur without erotic arousal, purely as an expression of aggression.

Wickler compares the straddled guard-posture of the monkey with the *herma* in front of the Greek house. He also offers the information that in Timor, Celebes, Borneo and Nias, wooden pillars are found of the same shape as the *herma* with a head and a phallos, but no arms or legs (Figure 27).

In the following chapter I shall show how a similar pattern

exists in humans and how its meaning corresponds to that of
the mounting-presentation signals in monkeys.

NOTES

1. S. Zuckermann, *The Social Life of Monkeys and Apes* (London, 1932),
    especially chapters 15, 16 and 17 (2nd edition in preparation).
2. S. E. Washburn and Irvin de Vore, 'The Social Life of Baboons',
    Scientific American, 1961, 6, p. 52.
3. Wolfgang Wickler, *Zeitschrift für Tierpsychologie*, 1966, 23, p. 423.

5

The Meaning of the Word argr
in Old Norse

In modern Danish the word *arg* is an unspecific, deprecatory term. The old Norse words *argr*, *ragr* or *ergi* are quite unequivocal. In the words of Martin Larsen—a Norse philologist who made an excellent translation into Danish of the *Edda*★—*argr* is 'the crudest term of abuse in old Norse. Applied to a man it indicated not only that he was effeminate, but also that he submitted himself to being used sexually as a woman.' He adds that accusations of this kind 'were regarded in a most serious light, demonstrated by the ancient Norwegian and Icelandic laws'.[1]

The meaning of the word emerges clearly from the contexts in which it appears. In the first song of Helgi Hundingsbani†—one of the songs of the *Edda*, based upon the legends of the Volsungs— Helgi's brother Sinfjotli enters into angry dispute with his foe Gudmundr, before the battle. Sinfjotli heaps accusations on Gudmundr for being *argr*, saying that he is a disgusting hag who proffered himself to him for love's pleasure (stanza 38). In stanza 39 Sinfjotli protests that all the *einherjar* (Odin's warriors in Valhalla) fought with each other to win the love of Gudmundr. Finally he states that Gudmundr was pregnant with nine wolf

---

★ The *Edda* is a collection of poems relating Norse myths and legends. Authorities think they were given their present shape in the tenth century, but of course their content is much older, having been passed on by oral tradition.

† Meaning 'Helgi, who was the bane of — that is, who felled — Hunding.'

cubs and that he, Sinfjotli, was the father. (Helgi and Sinfjotli are *Ylvingar*, that is 'of the Wolf's kin'.)

Obviously it was disgraceful for a man in ancient Scandinavia to be another man's underdog and to be used sexually as a woman by him. On the other hand, it was not considered in the least shameful to be able to force another man into that position — on the contrary, it was something to brag about; and certainly it could never have been the intention of Sinfjotli to blame the *einherjar*. The distance between this attitude and our own is striking; we do not make any such distinction between the 'male' and the 'female' sodomite. The resemblance to the way in which animals behave, as discussed in the previous chapter, is clear too. Sinfjotli and Gudmundr show the same pattern as two baboons fighting over their status in the hierarchy. To be able to mount another man is an expression of superiority in strength and rank and so is honourable, while it is a sign of weakness and submission to be forced to present and be mounted, a cause of disgrace to a man, who feels he should be any man's equal or even his superior.

When viewed in this context, it is not difficult to understand why Thor was uneasy at the prospect of being clad as a bride in the likeness of Freya in order to get his hammer back from the *jötun* (giant) Thrymr:

> *Aesir* [gods] might call me *argr*,
> if I let myself be dressed in a bride's veil.

It is equally clear how insulting it was to Loki for Odin to say to him:

> Eight winters you were in the underworld,
> a lactating cow and a woman,
> and there you bore children,
> and in that I find the mark of one who is *argr*.

Njördr is similarly insulting when he addresses Loki thus:

But it is strange that an *argr Ass* [god]
came in here, one who bore children.

Loki* was *argr*. The *Aesir* were about to lose Freya to the
iötun who was building the wall around Valhalla for them. Following Loki's evil advice, they had promised to give Freya to
him, provided he finished the wall in time. As it seemed he
would be able to do so, Loki, faced with the wrath of the *Aesir*,
was forced to transform himself into a mare in heat, in order to
make off with the stallion which was pulling the stones over to
the wall for the *jötun*. The stallion ran away into the woods with
the mare, and the *jötun* was unable to finish the wall in time and
lost his reward. But Loki became pregnant with eight-footed
Sleipnir who was later to be Odin's horse. In the *Hyndlasong*,
stanza 41, it is related how Loki became pregnant and bore
witches.

The Sagas reflect the same attitude, expressed in the same words
as in the *Edda*. In the Saga of Njal, Höskuld has been killed in-
famously by Skarp Hedin and the other sons of Njal. Höskuld
was a son of Njal too, but born out of wedlock. However, Njal
recognized him and even made him a thegn,† thereby arousing
the jealousy of his half-brothers. The dead Höskuld's kinsmen on
his mother's side were powerful people in Iceland, and for fear of
the far-reaching consequences that a great feud might have, all
good men of Iceland banded together to arrange a reconciliation.
Apparently they were successful. It was agreed that a threefold
wergeld—an immense amount of goods—had to be paid for the
death of Höskuld. Many influential persons who were not Njal's
kin made their contributions for the sake of peace. Before leaving
the room where the big pile of goods lay, Njal added a woman's

* Loki is the typical trickster among the Norse gods.
† I have translated the Norse word *godi* as 'thegn' because it is much closer to the real
meaning of the *godi* than is the word 'priest' which is sometimes used in English translations
but is quite misleading. The *godi* was a chief and all chiefs also fulfilled the functions of
priests.

silk cloak and a pair of women's shoes into the bargain. Now all that remained, in accordance with the terms of the agreement, was for the *wergeld* to be accepted by Höskuld's kin, the sons of Sigfus. Flosi as their leader had to receive the *wergeld* from Skarp Hedin, foremost among the sons of Njal: Flosi now entered and looked at the money.

'It is a great sum and handsomely paid, as was to be expected,' he said. Then he picked up the silk cloak, waved it in the air, and asked whose contribution that might be. Nobody answered. Once more he waved the cloak, laughing harshly, and asked the same question. Again nobody answered. 'Am I to understand that none of you knows who owned this garment,' he said, 'or don't you dare to tell me?' 'Who do you think gave it?' Skarp Hedin asked. 'Now that you ask me,' Flosi said, 'I think it is your father, that beardless man as they call him. Few can tell from just looking at him whether he is a man or a woman!' 'To mock him, the old man! Nobody who wanted to pass as a real man ever did that before. It is obvious to anybody that he is a man since he fathered sons on his wife. And few of our kinsmen have been lying unavenged at our gate!' Then he took the cloak and instead he tossed a pair of woman's blue knickers to Flosi saying that he would need them more. 'Why should I need them?' Flosi asked. 'People say that you are the bride of the Troll of the Swine Mountain,' Skarp Hedin answered, 'and that he uses you as his wife every ninth night.' Then Flosi kicked at the pile of money and said that he would not take a penny of it. They would be satisfied with nothing short of blood-vengeance for the death of Höskuld. He would give no pledge of peace nor accept it. 'Now we are going home,' he said to the Sigfussons, 'and then let the same fate befall us all.'[2]

Thus the great drama of revenge was set in motion, leading to the killing of Njal, his wife Bergthora, and their sons by setting fire to Njal's house, which, in turn, was to lead to further acts of revenge.

From the words of Flosi and Skarp Hedin, as from those in the *Edda*, it is clear that the accusations of being *argr* and of lacking the power of procreation were closely interconnected.

Again it must be stressed that the disgrace lay in being *argr*. There was no shame attached to the dominating, conquering homosexual aspect. Later I shall show that this attitude is common in peoples with whom homosexuality exists among normal men. Therefore, a homosexual relationship would remain problem-free only where there was an accepted difference of rank between the two parties, based for instance on the youthfulness and immaturity of the submissive partner as with the Dorians and the Japanese.

The examples given above show that the attitude of the ancient Norsemen towards homosexuality among normal men was entirely different from ours. Of primary importance for them was the power balance between men. It might be given symbolic expression in sexual imagery, or it might be manifested in action. During a quarrel between Skarp Hedin and Thorkel Haak, a great warrior, Thorkel was seated against the wall in the centre of a bench, with his men on either side of him. Skarp Hedin was standing some distance apart, with his brothers and others of his kin around him. In the course of the quarrel Thorkel became so furious that he sprang to his feet, drew his *sax* (a single-edged sword) and prepared to run Skarp Hedin through. Skarp Hedin stood with his axe raised high, 'Then he pushed his brothers and Kari away, stalked towards Thorkel, and said, "Choose now, Thorkel! Either you sheathe your *sax*, or I plant my axe in your skull and split you in two down to the shoulders!" Thorkel sat down and put up his *sax*, and it was the first time in his life that such a thing happened to him, and the last, too.'[3] The insult to Flosi of having it said about him that he submitted to the phallus of the Troll of the Swine Mountain, and the humiliation to Thorkel of having to retire when confronted with the axe of Skarp Hedin, amount to the same thing. What is decisive is the implication of being inferior in power. The sexual imagery is employed in addressing Flosi because it provides that special emphasis which is inherent in any comprehensive symbol. I shall deal with our ideas on homosexuality at a later stage. Suffice it here to say that they have little in common with these, and their origin is quite different.

NOTES

1. Martin Larsen, *Den ældre Edda* (Copenhagen, 1943), I, p. 235 (comment on stanza 23 of the poem *Lokasenna*).
2. *Njal's Saga* (Harmondsworth, 1970).
3. Ibid.

6

Phallic Worship in Ancient Scandinavia

The phallus played a part in the cult in Scandinavia as far back as the early period of the Stone Age, as shown by Norwegian rock carvings. (See Figure 9.)[1]

From the Scandinavian Bronze Age — that is the millennium between about 1600 and 400 B.C. — a wealth of material has come down to us testifying to the central place of the phallic symbol in the cult of that entire period. During the Bronze Age, culture seems to have been highly developed and dominated by a splendour-loving nobility. Figure 10 shows a typical rock carving from that period found in Bohuslen in the southern part of Sweden which, until three hundred years ago, belonged to the kingdom of Denmark–Norway. The carving depicts most of the same objects that have been found in Denmark in graves or lying in marshes, where they were placed for cultic purposes; it shows the great holy bronze axe, the *lurs* (the long, bent bronze horns), the sun disc, the sword, the shield, the lance, the bow and arrow. There are also carvings of ships, and of the plough (see Figure 11). There are depictions of the Sacred Marriage (Figure 12), and carvings of horned figures. Bronze statuettes have been found of gods wearing horned helmets like the one from the Viksø find in Denmark. All these are represented over and over again in many rock carvings, in particular from the late Bronze Age.

There is one feature which all the male participants in the cultic scenes have in common: they are conspicuously phallic (the phallus is contrasted in these pictures with the sword, which points obliquely backwards and downwards). It is striking that the men are phallic regardless of their activity; whether bearing on high the holy axe or blowing the *lur*, while standing before the sun, or fighting, hunting or ploughing, whether on board ship or—not unnaturally—while celebrating the Sacred Marriage.

Even without our knowledge of psychology it would seem natural to see in these rock carvings object lessons in the manifold meanings of the phallic symbol. The phallus is associated with all kinds of objects, which are usually regarded in dreams, for instance, as phallic representations; the sword, the lance, the arrow, the horn, the plough, the ship, etc. All in all the phallus is associated with objects expressing power and personal endowment, with the sublime and the holy. The cultic significance of the axe and the phallus and the close connection between the two stand out clearly in Figure 13. It would be just as meaningful to say that the picture shows the axe to possess the power of a phallus as to say that the phallus is seen to have the power of an axe. Thus in visual terms many meanings are condensed into the image of a phallus. Fertility, however important, is only one of them and in many of its dimensions, in the power of fighting and of hunting or of sailing, for instance, there is no room for a sexual component at all.*

The phallus must have been a central symbol, uniting much of

---

* The symbolic complexity of the plough for the Greeks is seen for example in the following: 1. In the Attic wedding ceremony the expression 'ploughing legitimate children' is used (Menander, fragment 720). The plough here is a symbol of fertility; 2. In *Oedipus the King* by Sophocles, verse 1207 and 1211–12, *the chorus sings*:

> O Oedipus . . .
> how, O how, have the furrows ploughed
> by your father endured to bear you, poor wretch.

(David Grene's translation, in *The Greek Tragedies*, edited by David Grene and Richard Lattimore.) Here the plough is an erotic symbol; 3. Pausanius tells (I, 32, 5) that during the battle of Marathon (490 B.C.), the Athenians saw the hero Ecetlaeus at the head of the army mowing down the Persians using a plough as his weapon. In this context the symbol has an aggressive meaning.

importance, at the great annual festivals of the Scandinavian
Bronze Age, the most important probably taking place during the
winter and summer solstices when the year had to be set on its
right course.

Apart from representations of copulation there are not more
than one or two female figures fully drawn in the petroglyphs.
However, cup-marks are found everywhere in great numbers.
According to Glob, these may be interpreted as female symbols.[2]

Phallic worship persisted in Scandinavia throughout the Iron
Age. In the National Museum in Copenhagen there is a wooden
image of a phallic god from the Celtic Iron Age. Moreover the
Bauta-stones are regarded as phalli on philological as well as
archaeological grounds. These stones without inscriptions are
found throughout Scandinavia and date from the Bronze Age,
the Iron Age, and the Viking period. They are between four and
five metres high, standing vertically in the ground (see Figure
14). A Bauta-stone marks a grave and is a sign of commemora-
tion, or has itself been the object of a cult, on the evidence of the
votive gifts found superficially buried in the surrounding soil.
Often they have names, such as 'the man', 'the sword', 'the
arrow', or 'pighellen' (i.e. the phallic stone). This last name is Norwegian and it points, as indeed do the other names, towards a
phallic meaning. The name Bauta is thought to be derived from
a word meaning 'to thrust', of the same root as beytill = vingull =
phallus. The Bauta-stones possess the same significance as the
white stones found in graves dating from the early Iron Age.[3]

Phallic worship still held a prominent position even while
Scandinavia was being Christianized. In the middle of the
eleventh century, at a time when Sweden had not yet accepted
Christianity, Adam, Archbishop of Bremen in north-eastern
Germany, described the heathen temple in Uppsala.[4] He told how
within the temple stood images of the three main gods, Odin,
Thor, and Frey. The statue of Frey was equipped with a mighty

phallus — *cum ingenti priapo*. Figure 15 shows a phallic statuette of a god, probably Frey, from Sweden.

We are fortunate in having in the *Edda* a description of phallic worship at a lonely Norwegian farm around the time of the Christianization of the country. To be sure, the story was written as a testimony of the power of Holy King Olav to convert his people to the Christian faith, but it is likely that the tale and the poems preserved in it contain authentic remnants of ritual formulas.[5]

The story, called the *Song of Vølse*, centres on a peasant, his wife, son and daughter, their bondman and bondwoman, all living on an isolated farm. The peasant's stallion dies; the son cuts off the stallion's member, and the peasant's wife wraps it in linen with onions and herbs, to prevent it rotting, and puts it in her chest. Every evening she takes it out and worships it, always addressing the same dedicatory words to it, and the story goes, 'the devil made it swell and become stiff, so that it could stand with the woman as often as she wanted it.' At the evening meal it is passed around among the members of the household, from the wife to her husband, then to their son and daughter, bondman and bondwoman. Each of them recites a poem to it, always addressing it with the phrase, 'Receive from us, *Mörner*, the gift.'[6] These words are probably remnants of an old ritual formula. The meaning of the word *Mörner* is uncertain. It may be one of the names of Frey. It is known that, until recently, the Lapps sacrificed the phallus of the reindeer to Frey.[7]

On reading the *Song of Vølse* it is impossible not to be reminded of the phallic festival of Dicaeopolis in Aristophanes' *The Acharnians*. There are several similarities between the two works: the cultic festival of domestic life with husband, wife, children, and slaves as participants, the phallic image and the phallic song.

It is obvious that the housewife on the Norwegian farm took the role of the priestess of Frey. In the *Flateybook* (one of the main

Norse sources) there is a story of phallic worship in Sweden. A Norwegian, Gunnar Helming by name, is captured by the Swedes at the very time that the image of Frey is being carried from place to place to secure a good year. Gunnar Helming is given the task of acting the part of Frey each time the Sacred Marriage is celebrated, and he performs so well that the priestess becomes pregnant, to the satisfaction of all, since this was regarded as a good omen.

In Chapter 14 we will discuss remnants of phallic worship which persisted after Scandinavia had been Christianized.

NOTES

1. Guttorm Gjessing, *Norges Steinalder* (Oslo, 1945).
2. P. V. Glob, 'Helleristninger i Danmark', *Jutland Archaeological Society Publications*, vol. VII, with an English summary (1969).
3. *Kulturhistorisk Leksikon for Nordisk Middelalder* (*Encyclopedia of the History of the Culture of the Middle Ages in Scandinavia*), s.v. *Bautastein*.
4. Adam of Bremen, *The History of the Hamburg Archbishopry*, book IV, section XXVI.
5. Martin Larsen, *Den ældre Edda* (Copenhagen, 1943), I, p. 45.
6. Ibid.
7. Op. cit., IV, p. 250.

7

The Janus-face of Submission

In this chapter I shall try to throw more light on the different aspects of submission in humans and animals as described in the three previous chapters, and I shall add some observations taken from current clinical experience. The first chapter dealt with Dorian paiderasty, the essence of which may be summarized in the words of Symonds written in 1908: 'A passionate and enthusiastic attachment subsisting between man and youth, recognized by society and protected by opinion, which, though it was not free from sensuality, did not degenerate into mere licentiousness.'[1] Paiderasty served the highest goal — education (*paideia*). Eros was the medium of *paideia*, uniting tutor and pupil. The boy submitted and let himself be taken into the possession of the man. In the fourth and fifth chapter it was shown that receptive submission is symbolized in the position and attitude of a female willing to be mounted, this being the most condensed expression of submissiveness.

The natural inclination of boys towards phallic worship has been mentioned, but there were other factors which made it possible for a Dorian boy to accept extreme submission without injury to his self-esteem or feelings of humiliation — without feeling *argr*. One was the considerable difference in age and development between the boy and his *erastēs*; this made it natural for the boy to accept the submissive role. Moreover he was aware that this state of submission was temporary, even though it would last for some years, and that it would lead him to acquire qualities of manliness and nobility that could make him eventually the equal of any man.

In addition, there is a second, important factor. Our way of thinking is shaped by a society very different from that of the Dorians. For instance in our society connections between persons are looser, involve less obligation and change more frequently. This, together with our democratic outlook, makes it easy for us to overlook the dependence of the dominating older man on his younger partner. They were tied together in a pact equally compelling for both. It was the obligation of the *erastēs* always to be an outstanding and impeccable example to the boy. He should not commit any deed that would shame the boy. His total responsibility towards the boy made him dependent on the boy in ways far beyond the purely erotic. He was judged by the development and conduct of the boy. Even in regard to the bodily aspect of the relationship the boy could assert himself against his tutor. Ephorus relates how on returning from the two months' stay at the country estate of his lover immediately following his capture, a boy made known his views on the physical intimacies of his tutor's love-making. The law expressly gave this privilege to the boy in order that he might revenge himself and get rid of the lover if, for instance, force had been used on him.[2]

This illustrates the fact that relationships with pronounced supremacy–subordination characteristics may exist which are not based on the unilateral, unlimited predominance of one of the partners.

However, paiderastic relationships of a purely erotic nature and without ethical ballast were much more precarious, in Greece as everywhere else. If a man flaunted his superiority and behaved in a scornful or tactless way, the pride of the youth might be hurt, making him react with violence. The tyrant Periander rashly asked his *paidiká* whether he was not yet pregnant. In a fury the boy sprang to his feet and killed him.[3] He reacted in this way because Periander hinted that he was *argr*. This would hardly have happened in a genuine *paidea*-relationship focused on the education of the youth.

There is also a third point to be taken into consideration. The Hellenes did not regard the genitals as a *pudendum* — as something to be ashamed of and to be covered up. The Greek word designating the attitude to the genital, *aidōs*, means awe before that which is sacred. It indicates the natural attitude to a symbol with the cultic significance of a phallus. The symbolic role played by the phallus of the older man for the boy as the incarnate giver of *aretē* — a view shared by the world around him — made his submission quite other than shameful and humiliating.

The situation was totally different in the case of grown equals, however. Whereas the Dorian boy would attain manhood through his submission, the grown man who submitted to another man would lose his manliness and become effeminate, exposed to shame and scorn. The ancient Greek reacted to this in the same way as the ancient Norseman: such a man became *argr*. This is what happened to the young king Pentheus of Thebes in Euripides' great tragedy, *The Bacchae*. Pentheus, a masterful and virile young man, witnesses with disgust how his city is being invaded by Dionysus and his train of *Bacchae*. They seduce most of the women of Thebes, including Pentheus' own mother, into leaving the city to go up on to Mount Cithaeron. Here, revelling in the whirling dances, the women abandon themselves to wild, ecstatic orgies. Clad in the cultic apparel of the god Dionysus, wrapped in fawn skin fastened with live snakes, with ivy in their hair and the *thyrsus* — a stalk of fennel tipped with ivy — in their hand (the *Bacchae* appear thus on numerous red-figure vases of the fifth century B.C.) they roam the mountains, tearing asunder all, humans or animals, who come in their way. Pentheus wants to free his country of all this. Not realizing that Dionysus is a god, he decides to take him prisoner and put an end to the orgies by

force of arms. The climax of the drama comes when a quarrel
breaks out between the god and the king. Pentheus begins power-
fully enough, while Dionysus, wearing a smiling mask, his long
yellow curls falling to his shoulders, apparently yields, and suffers
Pentheus to cut off his long hair. Presently, however, the roles
shift. Dionysus proves stronger and stronger, Pentheus comes
more and more under his influence and becomes increasingly
insecure. Finally he makes an attempt to collect himself and
resolutely gives an order for his armour to be brought to him.
But at this point a single expression of forceful firmness on the
part of Dionysus is enough to break down Pentheus' resistance
completely. Lured, fooled and seduced Pentheus now permits
himself to be dressed in the garments of the *Bacchae*, which
Dionysus actually helps him to put on. That Pentheus feels
debased by having to wear woman's clothes is brought out
strongly in his repeated attempts to protest (lines 823, 828, and
835) — he reacts exactly as Thor did, when Loki dressed him in
Freya's clothes — and also in the passage (line 850 ff.) in which
Dionysus says that he will have to strike Pentheus with madness,
because otherwise this man will never wear women's clothes.
There is later a detailed description (lines 925-39) of how in his
final state of submission Pentheus behaves effeminately and coyly
towards Dionysus. He has become completely *argr*. Now he
willingly follows Dionysus to Mount Cithaeron to meet his
dreadful fate — to be torn to pieces by the reckless and dazzled
Bacchae led by his own mother. But it is only his life he loses
there. The worst had already happened to him when he ceased
to be a man, losing his manhood to the very person he tried to
conquer.

   Pentheus' plight vividly echoes the grown man's fear of being
forced into the abased position of homosexual submission by
another man. We find the same attitude in any boy who feels
insulted at being called a cissy. These feelings are shared by the
Japanese who, having seen inverse homosexual relationships in

America or Europe with a 'male' and a 'female' partner, consider it shocking that one grown man should suffer himself to be cast in the submissive 'passive' role. They regard this as incompatible with a grown man's dignity. Not that the Japanese have anything against homosexual relationships as such — they occur among normal men in Japan — but they seek out boys as partners,[4] as the Greeks did.

A similar attitude — of contempt and disgust towards everything implied by the Norse word *argr* — is implicit, but rarely explicit, in our ordinary daily life. It is significant that the word is preserved in modern Danish, but has lost its specific meaning. Probably this is a direct consequence of the fact that grown men in Europe and North America do not recognize homosexual components in themselves.

Euripides conveyed the idea of *argr*-ness by portraying a normal man exposed to an extraordinary strain, overwhelming enough to make his personality crack and fall apart. In contemporary society, a man thrown out of psychic balance by inner disharmony can experience the panicky fear of being *argr* in a similar way. This is seen in males who suffer from disturbances of their potency, with the accompanying feeling of reduced self-confidence and vitality. This is the case too with states of powerlessness primarily non-sexual in origin. It may emerge with particular clarity in the course of psychotherapy with a male therapist. The examples which follow have not been selected in any way for their rarity; on the contrary, they are typical of that which, in one form or another, exists beneath the surface of all men.

A man in his early thirties came into treatment on account of a potency disturbance, not too severe, but troublesome nevertheless. Although he was heterosexually oriented, and had never been conscious of homosexual inclinations, he had a vague feeling that other people might find something 'homosexual' about him. Besides, he believed that his penis was smaller than other men's. He expected a lot from the treatment, and he expressed great

confidence in me. However, it was obvious from the very beginning that he was tense in my presence. Soon it was evident that
he was feeling insecure about involving himself in that relationship of one-sided dependency inherent in a psychotherapeutic
situation. He became afraid of having to deliver himself up to me
to the extent which is inevitable for a patient who has to come
several times a week and relate openly and without reservations
what he thinks, feels, and does. Then, very soon after the start of
the treatment he dreamt that he was standing before me in my
office without his pants on. He was in a state of violent agitation
and had a gun in his hand. He cried out, 'If you say I am a homosexual, then ... ', and then he shot me, waking up immediately
afterwards with strong anxiety. The dream showed why he was
tense and afraid of me. He feared that, insecure and in a state of
disturbed potency as he was, I should regard him as one who was
only half a man, and, taking advantage of his weakness, treat him
accordingly. This was what he defended himself against by shoot-
ing me. His fear of making a homosexual impression or – which
amounts to the same thing – that his penis was too small, covered,
as always in these cases, anxious feelings of somehow being *argr*.

Another man, forty years of age, sought my help because of
serious psychic disturbances. He had had several psychotic episodes, severe but transitory. Nevertheless, he was a highly gifted
person, and he made an important contribution within his field.
He was heterosexual. During the first sessions he appeared tense
and silent in spite of his evident wish to be helped. Apparently he
was distrustful. This continued until at last I succeeded in making
him speak. Hesitatingly at first, obviously fearful of my reaction,
he then revealed that he believed it to be my plan of treatment to
submit him to anal intercourse. Naturally he knew that my in-
tentions were of the best, but he was afraid of them. As I succeeded in convincing him that I had other means at my disposal
he quietened down. It was evident that my patient held a belief
similar to that of a Dorian boy. The latter was firmly convinced

that *aretē* was infused into him by his *erastēs*. My patient expected to be subjected to a transfer of sanity from me in a like manner. The difference is equally obvious: in Dorian Greece the paiderasty was in accord with the culture as a whole, therefore it was conflict-free, unlike the present-day situation. In addition everything connected with dominance-submission in this patient's disharmonious personality was complicated by sado-masochistic impulses charged with guilt, fear and shame, making him shy away from any intimate human relationship. The fundamental idea, however, was common to both patient and Dorian boy.

It is possible to give many more examples even without including cases whose symbolism needs interpretation, but one more will suffice.

A thirty-two-year-old man was referred to me for treatment on account of a spastic torticollis: against his will, his head jerked to the left in a spasmodic way. He was a musician, and played a wind instrument, so he was completely prevented from working by this symptom. He had no bodily ailment; the spasms were purely nervous. For several months before the appearance of his symptoms he had been practising rigorously in order to qualify for a distinguished appointment as a soloist with a particular orchestra. Secretly, however, he had great fears that he might not be able to live up to this position. Therefore he sought the help of an older colleague, a kind and solicitous friend who did all he could to support him. In his state of insecurity the patient chose to give up his own playing technique in favour of that of his colleague, in spite of the fact that it was very different from his own. He got the appointment. However, at the first performance in which he had to play solo, the spasmodic jerking appeared. He became completely incapacitated and remained so for nine months before coming to me for psychotherapy. The episodes that follow illustrate the typical problems lying at the core of his nervous condition. They also indicate the direction of the therapeutic work which eventually led to his recovery without the use of drugs.

Some time after the commencement of treatment he related a dream in which he saw his helpful colleague walking down the street leading a small monkey by the hand. The monkey toddled obediently along beside his colleague, looking up at the big man. I asked the patient whether the dream meant anything to him. After a short deliberation he replied that he was the small monkey. After all he aped his colleague by adopting his technique of playing. Up until then I had not commented on his dependency on this colleague, but from then on and for a long time afterwards it became one of the main themes in the treatment. The dream had quite clearly illustrated what had taken place in this relationship. During the period that followed, there emerged detail by detail, a picture of how completely he had given up his own personal style of playing—the make of instrument, the kind of mouth-piece, the method of blowing, and so forth—in order to borrow the strength and capability of the other man by imitation. In this way he assumed a manner of playing which was not his own, and which did not prove fit for him. Besides, he had accepted a degree of subordination wounding to his pride and his feeling of masculinity. As long as he felt he could not do without help, he put up with this state of dependence. But no sooner had he got his appointment than his wish to assert himself and to be his own master flared up aggressively.

His submission to his colleague as well as his passionate wish to free himself of this dependence contained repetitive elements from unresolved conflicts in his relationship with his father. These old conflicts, aroused by the present situation, resulted in a state of strong inner disharmony and tension which manifested itself outwardly in his nervous symptom.

After the subject of dependence had been opened up light was thrown on it by a series of dreams. In one of them his colleague repeatedly jumped on his back crying out triumphantly. At the end of the dream the patient knocked him down, and then awoke, feeling uneasy. The earlier 'aping' dream showed him 'presenting'; in this he was being mounted by the older man, to which he reacted with fearful aggression.

Soon the same theme came to the fore in his relationship with me. A treatment situation is also an apprenticeship, and it became increasingly apparent that he felt himself to be in a state of submission to me. This was frightening because, constrained by his suffering and his disability, he felt caught in the dependence. This fear was given expression in many ways. For instance he dreamt that he was taking his three-year-old boy to the doctor, who was sitting with the boy in his lap. To the deep concern of the patient the doctor started playing with the boy's penis. When asked by the patient why he was doing this, the doctor answered, 'It is my right to take my pleasure too.' Judging from the situation as a whole—the dream, his attitude to me and many things he had said and done during the treatment—it was beyond doubt that I was the doctor. So the patient's little son was an extension of himself, and both the penis of the boy and the whole boy stood for the patient's penis and himself as a whole. Just a hint from me made him see the dream in this light. Thereupon, haltingly and with many pauses, he confessed to wanting for some time to ask me whether I found anything 'homosexual' about him. He had the feeling that maybe other people saw him in this way. It was impossible for him to tell what exactly might make this impression on others. He did not feel any attraction towards other men, nor was he aware of feminine traits in himself, but nevertheless... (In reality the patient was a virile type and clearly heterosexual.) He then added that his wife could not reach orgasm except through clitoral stimulation, and maybe that was his fault, because he was not a real man ... He did not feel his potency to be disturbed nor did he have difficulty in maintaining intercourse pleasurably over a reasonable period of time. It was just that his wife achieved no satisfaction that way. She, for her part, had no complaints against him, and although they had talked about it, this had been of no help to him.

In the misery of his insecurity this man gave himself up to a *paidea*-relationship with an older colleague, sacrificing his autonomy to partake of the stronger man's ability. He tolerated this position as long as no other way seemed possible. However, being a grown man, with an ambition to rank as an equal of the best, a strong conflict was aroused in him resulting in his breakdown. His situation, caricatured in the dream image of the 'aping', clearly demonstrates how submission may be a road to identification with a stronger person; and both the signals of presentation and of mounting appear in his dreams. The same applies to his therapeutic relationship to me: he felt homosexual submission to be the price of recovery. To him, as to other men, the idea of making a 'homosexual' impression was tantamount to the fear of being regarded as *argr* — as a man unable to assert himself on equal footing with other men.

The examples given illustrate the existence, just beneath the surface of consciousness, of rooted patterns, which we have the honour of sharing with our ancestors.

Two thousand years ago these radicals were not hidden, but were proclaimed in the streets and market-places. At Caesar's triumphal entry into Rome after the Gallic War the legionaries following his carriage chanted pasquinades about him, as was their right on such occasions. One of the pasquinades went along the lines that just as Caesar had subdued Gaul so Nicomedes had subdued Caesar. What they were referring to was that Caesar, at the age of twenty, when already an officer of the Roman army, had had a love affair with King Nicomedes of Bethynia, in which he was the submissive partner. He never heard the last of it. Often he was named 'Nicomedes's queen', and Suetonius calls it 'a serious and lasting stain on his reputation, provoking universal scorn'. Cicero is said to have referred to this relationship in his letters and to have teased Caesar with it in the Senate. On one occasion a senator insultingly called him a woman, and Caesar's insignificant co-consul Bibulus referred to Caesar as 'the queen of Bethynia' in his edicts.[5] The reason why they scoffed at him was that as a grown man, and a Roman army officer, he had taken the 'female' position with another man. Nobody would have thought of teasing him because he had relationships with boys.

It is essential to remember that Caesar was not an inverse homosexual in the sense that we understand that expression. He had numerous relationships with women. The older Curio called him 'the husband of all wives and wife of all husbands'. During the same triumphal entry in which the soldiers taunted Caesar over his old relationship with Nicomedes, they also chanted, 'Citizens guard your wives, here comes the bald lecher. All the money he borrowed in Rome he wasted on women in Gaul.'[6] It is well known that once he ran the risk of political ruin because he was unable to part from a woman — Cleopatra of Egypt, who had a son by him.

The legionaries' scoffing and the many other insults he had to endure in connection with the Nicomedes affair — Cicero's in the Senate, for instance — again show that certain relationships which appear to us simply as sexual were regarded by the ancients as expressions of dominance or submission: falling, that is, within the sphere of aggression. Accordingly the imputation was that Caesar was *argr*, the underdog of another man. Dio Cassius relates that Caesar bore all the teasings of the soldiers in good spirit except for their references to his relationship with Nicomedes. These he took hard, and tried to repudiate the charge by taking an oath, only making himself the more ridiculous thereby.[7] It shows us a point of view which, like that of the ancient Scandinavians, is far removed from our own moralistic attitude to sex.

So submission may be accepted and valued in certain roles — that of the pupil, for instance — while under other circumstances it is considered shameful and debasing, as with Pentheus and with Caesar. The conflict of having at the same time a strong need for

G

submission and a deadly fear of it is exemplified in the reactions of my own patients who feel compelled by their suffering and their disabilities to accept the fearful but necessary therapeutic apprenticeship with me. These cases demonstrate the Janus-faced ambiguity of the nature of submission.

This ambiguity is obvious, too, in societies depending on a hierarchy for their stability and ability to survive. Among baboons those who are inferior in rank are subdued and sexually inhibited. At the same time, their state of submission is one of the links which bind the troop together as an organized whole, providing peace, leadership and protection. It is not difficult to find parallels in man, from the most 'primitive' societies up to the highly organized feudal states. In the latter, symbolic signals of mounting and presentation can be seen in the ancient ceremonies involving rank. A vassal paid homage to his liege by taking the oath. He placed his hand on the point of his lord's sword, while being himself unprotected; in other words, he delivered himself up unconditionally. When a vassal was to receive the accolade, he knelt with head bowed, in a position reminiscent of the presentation, while the lord let fall his naked sword on the vassal's shoulder. This is not unlike the submissive wolf offering its vulnerable neck to its superior.

The multiple aspects of subordination and dominance are apparent in these cases. However, what is also clear is that the dependence is not one-sided. It is just as binding on the dominating as the subordinate partner. Liege lords as well as dominating baboons have far-reaching obligations towards those subordinate to them in rank, and if they do not live up to these obligations they eventually lose their dominance. This mutual dependence between lord and people runs through medieval history, as the Danish historian Aksel E. Christensen has pointed out. Discussing a pact which was made in 1360 between the Danish King Waldemar IV, a powerful ruler, and his people, Christensen mentions that ' ... transgression of the pact would make the king "a tyrant" by which, according to common medieval thinking, he would automatically lose his right to the throne'.[8] A number of Danish kings were taught this lesson. In about 1600, in the reign of the Spanish King Carl V, the Aragonian oath of homage still ran as follows: 'We who are every one of us just as much as thou, and who all of us together are more than thou, we make thee our king. If thou respectest our laws and privileges we obey thee; if thou doest not, we do not.'*[9]

I have dealt with submission in this chapter only as it pertains to men. The vaginally receptive role of the woman has indeed its submission-aspect — without it there can be no harmonious feminine function. However, the receptive element of femininity is far from being an expression of submission only. It has equally well the character of taking into possession. Examine, for instance, the Bronze Age depiction of copulation in Figure 12. The female partner shows no sign of being subdued and submissive, though of course it is the male partner who has the active penetrating role. These Bronze Age pictures, like burial customs from the Stone Age to the present day, are clear expressions of the equality of status which Scandinavian women have enjoyed throughout history. However, the order of dominance-submission among women and its management is outside the scope of this book.

NOTES

1. John Addington Symonds, *A Problem in Greek Ethics* (London, 1908).
2. Strabo, 10, 4, 21.
3. Plutarch, The Dialogue on Love, *Moralia* 768 F.
4. Ruth Benedict, *The Chrysanthemum and the Sword* (Boston, 1967), p. 188.
5. Suetonius, *The Twelve Caesars*, chs. 2, 49.

* The economic and the social aspects of the liege-vassal relationship went hand in hand, reinforcing one another.

6. Op. cit., ch. 50.
7. Dio Cassius, book 43, chs. 20, 2.
8. Aksel E. Christensen, *Kongemagt og Aristokrati* (*Kingdom and Aristocracy*) (Copenhagen, 1968), p. 200. First edition 1945.
9. Ludwig Pfandl, *Philipp II* (Munich, 1938), p. 128.

8

Phallic Aggression

Sir Richard Burton, who issued his great translation of *The Arabian Nights* in the 1880s, knew life in the Near East as few have done. After serving as an army officer in India, he went to Arabia, where he absorbed the way of life to such a point that he ventured on a pilgrimage to Mecca, saw the Kaba, and escaped unscathed — an adventure with more than life at stake, for had he been detected death would not have been the worst fate awaiting him. However, he had become such a respected figure that afterwards no grudge was borne against him in the Arab world.[1] He knew Persia too. In his 'terminal essay' to *The Arabian Nights* he writes:

> A favourite Persian punishment for strangers caught in the *Harem* or *Gynæceum* is to strip and throw them and expose them to the embraces of the grooms and Negro slaves. I once asked a *Shirazi* how penetration was possible if the patient resisted with all the force of the sphincter muscle: he smiled and said, 'Ah, we Persians know a trick to get over that: we apply a sharpened tent-peg to the crupper-bone and knock, till he opens.' A well-known missionary to the East during the last generation was subjected to this gross insult by one of the Persian Prince-governors, whom he had infuriated by his conversion mania: in his memoirs he alludes to it by mentioning his 'dishonoured person'; but English readers cannot comprehend the full significance of the confession.[2]

The dishonour which, as Burton rightly says, his countrymen could not fully appreciate, would have been perfectly well understood by a Norseman. The man had been made *argr*.

Burton's story as well as other reports — both past and present — from the Near East of men being raped make it clear that those responsible are not simply members of some unusual, perverted minority. Alien as these phenomena appear to our thinking and imagination, we have to ask how in such circumstances it is psychophysiologically possible for a man to produce an erection which is strong enough for penetration. According to the ideas current in our part of the world, only erotic stimuli are capable of inducing erection. However, it is impossible that the grooms of the Persian prince could have been erotically aroused by every single violator of a harem or missionary with a religious conversion mania.

It appears, then, that emotions and impulses other than erotic ones may cause erection and genital activity in men; just as, in the baboon, mounting and penetrating to show superiority, or sitting on guard with legs apart and penis threateningly exposed show erection of an asexual origin. Correspondingly the belief of the Norseman in his ability to exert phallic dominance over an enemy by making him *argr* is likely to have found some expression in his physiology too. The same will probably have been the case with the Bronze Age people of Scandinavia — or of northern Italy for that matter — since they equated phallic power with the power of the spear, the sword and the axe, as we can see from their petroglyphs.

We have to conclude, therefore, that different varieties of effect derived from what we call aggression may be able to act as stimuli of erection and genital activity in men — the triumphant pleasure of subduing and humiliating another man, for instance. The aggressive element, void of all erotism, is precisely what is operating in such scenes of collective violence as that described in the biblical tale of Sodom:

And there came two angels to Sodom at even; and Lot sat in
the gate of Sodom; and Lot seeing them rose up to meet
them; and he bowed himself with his face toward the
ground; and he said, Behold now, my lords, turn in, I pray
you, into your servant's house, and tarry all night, and wash
your feet, and ye shall rise up early, and go on your ways.
And they said, Nay; but we will abide in the street all
night. And he pressed upon them greatly; and they turned
in unto him, and entered into his house; and he made
them a feast, and did bake unleavened bread, and they did
eat.

But before they lay down, the men of the city, even the
men of Sodom, compassed the house round, both old and
young, all the people from every quarter: and they called
unto Lot, and said unto him, Where are the men which
came in to thee this night? Bring them out unto us, that we
may know them. And Lot went out at the door unto them,
and shut the door after him, and said, I pray you, brethren,
do not so wickedly. Behold now, I have two daughters which
have not known man; let me, I pray you, bring them out
unto you, and do ye to them as is good in your eyes: only
unto these men do nothing; for therefore came they under
the shadow of my roof. And they said, Stand back. And they
said again, This one fellow came in to sojourn, and he will
needs be a judge: now will we deal worse with thee, than
with them. And they pressed sore upon the man, even Lot,
and came near to break the door. But the men put forth
their hand, and pulled Lot into the house to them, and shut
to the door. And they smote the men that were at the door
of the house with blindness, both small and great: so that they
wearied themselves to find the door.[3]

The pleasure that the men of the city, 'even the men of
Sodom—both old and young', wanted to achieve by 'knowing'

the two men was an aggressive pleasure. It is meaningless to speak
of anything erotic in connection with this attempt at anal rape,
or with any other such manifestations of collective violence.

When, in 1453, Constantinople fell to the Turks, Sultan
Mehmet first thought of making Lucas Notaras governor of the
conquered city. Notaras, who had been the *Megadux*, that is,
commander-in-chief of the army, was one of the most distinguished of the surviving Byzantine dignitaries. Distrustful, as
Mehmet always was, he wanted to test Notaras' loyalty or, to
put it more accurately, he wished to see proof that Notaras was
willing to submit to him totally and unconditionally. Pederasty
had always been one of the erotic enjoyments of the Turks, and
from the captured noble Byzantines Mehmet reserved the fairest
of the young sons as well as daughters for his seraglio.[4] To the
Christian sodomy was a sin, an enormity, and a horror. Here in
Sir Steven Runciman's words is what was asked of Notaras by
Mehmet:

> ... counsellors warned him (Mehmet) not to trust the
> Megadux. He put his loyalty to the test. Five days after the
> fall of the city he gave a banquet. In the course of it, when
> he was well flushed with wine, someone whispered to him
> that Notaras' fourteen-year-old son was a boy of exceptional
> beauty. The Sultan at once sent a eunuch to the house of
> the Megadux to demand that the boy be sent to him for
> his pleasure. Notaras, whose two elder sons had been killed
> fighting, refused to sacrifice the boy to such a fate. Police
> were then sent to bring Notaras with his son and his young
> son-in-law, the son of the Grand Domestic Andronicus
> Cantacuzenus, into the Sultan's presence. When Notaras still
> defied the Sultan, orders were given for him and the two
> boys to be decapitated on the spot. Notaras merely asked
> that they should be slain before him, lest the sight of his

death should make them waver. When they had both perished he bared his neck to the executioner.[5]

It is clear that Mehmet was not motivated by erotism in the true sense of the word. What he wanted was to see the most extreme sign of submission on the part of Notaras, as would have been the case had he abandoned his young son to the sodomy of Mehmet.

Four and a half centuries later a Turkish magistrate acted in a similar manner towards a man from the Christian world — Lawrence of Arabia — but this time the victim did not save his honour as Notaras had done. In 1917, Lawrence sneaked into Deraa, an area occupied by the Turks, as a spy. However, two Arabs betrayed him, informing the Turks that he would be coming and describing his disguise. He was taken prisoner and brought to the Turkish governor Hajim Bey who at once demanded that Lawrence place himself at his disposal sodomitically. Lawrence refused, but the guard threw him on a bench and lashed him until the pain 'which wrapped itself like a flaming wire about my body' made him surrender to Hajim Bey. Strangely enough, he succeeded in escaping from Deraa that same night. He himself explains that the guards were careless, believing him to be more seriously injured than he was. The Turkish governor concealed the episode for fear of reprisals from his superiors because of Lawrence's escape. However, the two treacherous Arabs learned what had happened between Hajim Bey and Lawrence, and spread it abroad, causing irreparable harm to Lawrence's reputation in the Arab world, which in turn had political repercussions. Even during the negotiations at Versailles, for instance, the story is said to have been revived. In a letter to Mrs Bernard Shaw dated March 26th 1924, Lawrence relates the events of the night in Deraa and the effect it had on him:

You instance my night in Deraa, well I'm always afraid of being hurt and to me, while I live, the force of that night will be in the agony that broke me, and made me surrender ... About that night, I shouldn't tell you, because decent men don't talk about such things. I wanted to put it plain in the book, and wrestled for days with my self respect ... which wouldn't, hasn't let me. For fear of being hurt, or rather to earn five minutes' respite from a pain which drove me mad, I gave away the only possession which we are born into the world with — our bodily integrity. It's an unforgivable matter, an irrecoverable position: and it's that which has made me forswear decent living, and the exercise of my not contemptible wits and talents. You may call this morbid; but think of the offence, and the intensity of my brooding over it for these years. It will hang about me whilst I live, and afterwards if our personality survives. Consider wandering among the decent Ghosts hereafter, crying 'unclean, unclean!'[Figure 16][6]

So the rape of Lawrence by the Turk that night in Deraa became the turning point in his life, forcing him to leave behind everything belonging to his previous existence and to renounce his position and titles in order to hide in the anonymity of the rank and file.

In their book, *The Secret Lives of Lawrence of Arabia*, Simpson and Knightley wonder why Lawrence was unable to shake off the ignominy of an experience against which he had been powerless to defend himself, and for which, therefore, he could have had no responsibility. They seem to forget that at that time Lawrence's world was the Arab world. As the Arabs and indeed Lawrence himself saw it, he should have done as Notaros did. The right thing would have been to bear the pain, no matter how long and severe, even at the cost of his life. This is difficult for us to understand, but the Norsemen would have agreed: be tortured to death rather than give in and become *argr*. It is an old and deeply ingrained pattern of response which comes to light in Lawrence.

I have said of the men of Sodom, of the grooms of the Persian prince, of Mehmet and of Hajim Bey that their zest for violent anal penetration had as its driving force aggression, not erotism. This does not mean of course that no pleasure is derived from the orgasm resulting from such violence. But primarily it is not connected with erotic feelings—it is not the expression of warmth and the urge for union, for giving as well as for taking, for being possessed as well as for possessing. It is primarily a release of aggressive tension, of the urge to exert power, to subdue, to humiliate and emasculate the victim. The baboon sitting on guard with an erect penis demonstrates the prototypical aggressive erection, and if he mounts a surrendering foe and effects anal penetration this, again, is by means of an erection due to aggressive stimuli. Clinical experience with human males shows, too, that there is a difference between the predominantly aggressive orgastic pleasure and that which is the outcome of a synthesis of love with a tempered aggression.

According to Lawrence it was common in the Turkish army for the officers to force sodomitic acts upon their subordinate soldiers. This made, he says, 'the thought of military service in the Turkish army a living death for wholesome Arab peasants'.

These different examples of phallic aggression reveal features of a pattern deeply ingrained in human and animal nature. Aggressiveness may be an effective stimulus for erection and peno-anal activity. Nevertheless, the very idea of aggressive expression in this form is remote from our way of thinking. It can fairly be said that the average grown man in our society would prove incapable of actions such as those performed by the Persian grooms. All the same, as we have seen from the examples given in the previous chapter, it is not difficult to establish the

existence of the same radicals in men of today under the surface
of their waking consciousness.

To this could be added further conclusions drawn from observations made in recent research into sleep patterns. A few years
ago it was noticed that during the sleep of normal persons there
are periods of complete rest and other periods when the eyeballs
move behind the closed lids. If a person is woken while his eyes
are at rest he will have no dream to relate; however, if wakened
during a period of eye activity he comes right out of a dream.
This pattern has occurred so consistently that it is now regarded
as an established fact that when there is eye-movement the
sleeper will be dreaming. Further it has been shown from ence-
phalographic records that the electrical activity of the brain during
the quiet phases when people do not dream is quite different
from that during the periods with eye movement and dream
activity. During the dream phases irregularities occur in pulse-
beat, respiration and blood-pressure, and small jerky movements
of the muscles are observed. Usually a night's sleep comprises
four to five dream phases; together they occupy approximately
one fifth of the sleep period.

Erections occur too during the dream phases. It is well known
that men frequently wake up in the morning with an erection,
and a strong erection at that; but more often than not these
erections, though not unpleasurable in a general way, are un-
accompanied by erotic sensations or thoughts. When a person
wakes up spontaneously it is most frequently from a dream
phase. However, total or partial erection occurs during the earlier
dream phases of the night also; so that in fact the sleeping male
has erections during a not inconsiderable part of the time he is
asleep. The first dream phase appears one to one and a half hours
after falling asleep. The erections may of course occur as an
accompaniment to erotic dreams. But the dream content is not
predominantly of an erotic nature, even though an erection is
present. Erection and seminal emission have been observed not

infrequently in association with aggressive or fearful dream situations. Erection may be present also during dreams of successful, non-sexual achievement. So erection takes place in many kinds of dream situations.[7]

We may compare the erection occurring during sleep in connection with asexual dreams with the Bronze Age petroglyphs of Figures 9, 10 and 11 and the commentaries in the text. A petroglyph also contains imagery, expressing, like the dream, figures and events from our inner world seldom nowadays displayed openly in waking consciousness. In the pictures of these rock carvings erection appears, as in dreams, in association with sexual and aggressive scenes and in addition with other activities such as sailing, ploughing and hunting which can be regarded as expressions of male powerfulness and capability in the widest sense, but which are neither directly sexual nor aggressive.

The small bushmen of South Africa depict themselves in their rock paintings with erect penes. In fact it appears that many of them are in a constant state of partial erection throughout the day—a phenomenon they display with pride.[8, 9]

According to the views of various competent anatomists whom I have consulted there is no known anatomical or physiological explanation for this. It might be conceivable, then, that in these small, extremely virile men the mechanism of erection is continuously open to stimuli from their inner world of feeling and imagination, with the consequence that the proud self-assurance, said to be so typical of them, causes a non-erotic state of genital excitement the whole day. In this event they would be, throughout the day, in the same psycho-physiological state as the males of our society during their dream phases or as the monkeys when threatening.

In this chapter I have stressed the phallic-aggressive meaning which erection may have, especially in homosexual contexts. This is not, however, to exclude the heterosexual relationship,

where phallic aggression may be seen in strongly self-assertive
men who hunt down women to show off their conquering
masculinity while at the same time lacking genuine erotic feelings
and the ability to abandon themselves to a woman. Wilhelm
Reich was the first to categorize this type of man, under the term
'phallic narcissism'.[10] It is well illustrated in the case of a patient
of mine who came into treatment because he was unable to form
a lasting connection with a woman. He had had numerous liaisons,
but as soon as marriage seemed to be approaching, he would take
flight, though he could find no fault with the girl. Soon he
would find another one and start all over again. He had problems
in his relations with other men, as well. He was unusually gifted
and intelligent, a forceful person, extremely successful, dominating most of the men in his circle. However, he would too
easily become distrustful, feeling provoked or threatened for no
good reason. He would therefore fight unnecessary battles, and
could be unreasonably harsh to men working under him. The
phallic expression of his over-emphasized aggressiveness and the
inner conflicts connected with it came to the fore in his dreams,
of which this is one: a man was standing with his back to him
some distance away, a big man, of repulsive appearance. He was
infuriated by the sight of the man, and feeling hate and contempt
for him he approached him from behind and thrust his index
finger into the man's anus (the man was fully dressed, but dreams
have a way of ignoring such details). At the same time a warning
voice was heard saying, 'Beware, he might break your finger'.
The patient added that these words recalled to him a visit years
ago to a friend who was then a medical student. His friend told
him that at the hospital he had been shown how to examine the
prostate gland of a man. You push your index finger up the
patient's anus and feel the gland. The instructor specifically emphasized the importance of pressing the left arm firmly against
the bowed back of the patient, lest by straightening up suddenly
the patient might break the index finger. (If in fact the instructor

actually did give this advice, it tells one more of his fantasies than of any real danger in a prostate examination.) A number of details in the dream, the life history of the patient and his relations to me — circumstances I cannot go into for reasons of discretion — make it clear that the big, disgusting, potentially dangerous man in the dream is a compromise–image of his father and me. In this dream he expresses his wishes to conquer and humiliate both of us, his finger being a phallic representation. At the same time the dream is a picture of violent phallic dominance and of the anxiety connected with it. There is nothing erotic or libidinous in the dream.

For the sake of clarity I have deliberately chosen pure and un-alloyed examples of hostile, phallic aggressiveness. It is certainly not my intention to convey the idea that phallic activity as such is predominantly aggressive, but it should be stressed that the harmonious heterosexual activity of a man has to contain a strong element of aggression. Otherwise he will be unable to display enough energy and initiative to call up the full erotic response of a normal woman. However, this aggression is con-trolled, tempered and, most important, modified by the addition of love. On the whole a synthesis of libido and aggression is a precondition for harmonious functioning in any close relation-ship, heterosexual or homosexual, with or without genital in-volvement. Both the aggressive and the libidinous components are modified by this synthesis, a 'fusion' as it is generally called. The presence of both components may be evident, but it will not be possible to draw a sharp dividing line between them. Dorian paiderasty is an example of a *paideia*-relationship uniting Eros and aggression; both were visible, though each modified and was inseparable from the other. Indeed, in any fruitful teacher-pupil relationship, including those in cultures where the genital com-ponent is precluded, united — fused — aggression and libido would be at the core of the relationship.

NOTES

1. Lesley Blanch, *The Wilder Shores of Love* (London, 1954).
2. Richard Burton, *Thousand Nights and A Night*, Terminal Essay X (Benares, 1885), p. 235.
3. Genesis XIX.
4. Steven Runciman, *The Fall of Constantinople* (Cambridge, 1965), p. 149.
5. Op. cit., p. 151.
6. Colin Simpson and Phillip Knightley, *The Secret Lives of Lawrence of Arabia* (London and New York, 1969).
7. See, for instance, Ernest Hartmann, *The Biology of Dreaming* (Springfield, 1967).
8. I. Schapera, *The Khoisan Peoples of South Africa* (London, 1950), ch. 1.
9. Laurens van der Post, *The Lost World of the Kalahari* (London, 1950), ch. 1.
10. Wilhelm Reich, *Character Analysis* (London, 1940). First published in German 1933.

9

On the Anal Response

To many among us it is probably a strange notion, difficult to comprehend, that in a sodomitic relationship the anally receptive or 'passive' partner is capable of feeling pleasure or satisfaction. It might be thought quite simply that the anus and the rectum are not susceptible to erotic stimulation or to any kind of pleasurable stimulation at all. Besides, the feelings of disgust at faeces, with which these parts of the body are closely associated, are likely to be decisive in the attitude of many people towards any kind of anal practice. Our culture is a rather special one in this respect. Freud once let fall a remark to the effect that we should not take our own feelings of disgust at all things anal quite so much for granted. Begging not to be accused of partiality he remarks that the penis might be dismissed with disgust as a sexual organ on similar grounds, serving, as it does, for evacuation of urine. However, this attitude towards the male genital is held only by extraordinarily hysterical women.[1]

To the unbiased observer it is a universal rule that small children, from one and a half to five or six years of age, are vividly and pleasurably interested in their own anal region and those of other children. The smallest children are also attracted to faeces. Freud rightly describes the skin, the mucous membranes and the muscles of the ano-rectal region as an erogenous zone, a zone, that is, which is erotically sensitive. This anal interest persists for a time in the child, even when at three to five years of

H

age the focus of attention begins to shift to the genitals. It is only because of severe cultural pressures that infantile anal sensitivity retreats to such an extent that for many people it is replaced by a veritable ano-rectal anaesthesia with regard to pleasurable sensations.

It is worth remembering that to a large proportion of the world's people the idea of using the mouth for erotic pleasure is completely alien. In kissing we have preserved and cultivated an infantile sensitivity which they have discarded.

No doubt in cultures different from ours children may be brought up in a way which allows them to preserve a degree of ano-rectal sensitivity beyond the period of early childhood. Probably this was the case with the Dorians, and perhaps this aspect has not been sufficiently emphasized in my earlier descriptions of the erotic responsiveness of the Dorian boy. Similar conditions are bound to have prevailed in the Near East in former times as well as the present. To the erotic anal element should be added a particular emotional experience open to the 'passive' partner, pleasure from submission, which may be felt strongly in such situations, without masochism in the true sense of this term being involved.

Even in our civilization far more grown men and women than is generally believed include anal stimulation in their mutual caressing, without their sex life as a whole justifiably being called perverted. Even anal coitus fully carried out is not at all rare. This is testified to by the following passage in the Kinsey report on women: ' ... the receiving partner, female or male, often reports that the deep penetration of the rectum may bring satisfaction which is, in many respects, comparable to that which may be obtained from deep vaginal insertion.'[2] Some women also claim that they reach orgasm through anal intercourse. The frequency of anal intercourse between man and woman in a section of the population of Copenhagen is shown in a report of an investigation by Tage Jensen into the number of women infected by gonorrhoea who were treated at a public clinic over a period of two and a half years, from 1950 to 1952.[3] Most of them were younger working-class women. Nearly one third had a rectal infection. The majority were asked whether they had had anal intercourse, and half of them answered in the affirmative. The denials of the rest often made an evasive and unreliable impression, and the author concludes that it is most likely that they all contracted their rectal gonorrhoea through anal intercourse. Probably he is right, but in any case one sixth of the women with gonorrhoea admitted having had intercourse that way, so that this phenomenon cannot possibly be all that rare.

There are men who become sufficiently aroused through deep anal penetration to reach emission and orgasm without any further stimulation. According to Kinsey *et al.*, 'it is only an occasional individual who is brought to orgasm by such techniques'.[4] (The Kinsey method of interrogation may not be particularly suitable for extracting information about these matters.) Without looking for such cases I have met three of them during my years of clinical practice. In their appearance these men seemed masculine enough, and they did not show 'homosexual' mannerisms.

Non-perverted, heterosexual men in psychoanalytic treatment may experience spontaneous pleasurable ano-rectal sensations transitorily during a period after the working through and solution of submission conflicts in the relationship to the analyst.

Among monkeys and apes anal caressing is the rule during the pre-coital petting, regardless of sex.

NOTES

1. Sigmund Freud, *Three Contributions to the Theory of Sex*, Collected Works (London, 1953).
2. A. C. Kinsey, W. B. Pomeroy, C. E. Martin, P. H. Gebhard,

Sexual Behaviour in the Human Female (Philadelphia and London, 1953), p. 581.

3. Tage Jensen, *Ugeskrift for Læger* (1953), 115, p. 1614.

4. A. C. Kinsey, W. B. Pomeroy, C. E. Martin, *Sexual Behaviour in the Human Male* (Philadelphia and London, 1948), p. 579.

10

The Relationship between Peers

The ancient Mesopotamian heroic poems of Gilgamesh were written down in epic form in the seventh century B.C. Gilgamesh was a god and a human being at the same time, and he bullied the inhabitants of the city of Uruk to such an extent that they appealed to the gods for help. The mother goddess, Aruru, then created Enkidu, a creature half man and half bull. In order to be able to help mankind against Gilgamesh, Enkidu had to be humanized. So a courtesan was sent to him who, living with him for six days and seven nights, taught him human love, clad him in human garments, accustomed him to the bread and the wine of the land, alienated him from the animals, and made him follow her to Uruk. Here he met Gilgamesh who, as was his tyrannical custom, was about to usurp the place of a bridegroom at the side of his bride during their first night. Enkidu barred his way to the bridal chamber, and like two roaring bulls they charged each other. However, suddenly the wrath of Gilgamesh subsided, they kissed and concluded a pact of friendship. This was the fulfilment of two dreams which Gilgamesh once had and which his mother interpreted to him. In the first dream he saw a star descending upon him from heaven, and he says to his mother, 'I was drawn to it as though to a woman.' In the second dream he saw an axe, 'That axe, strange was its shape—I loved it, and as though to a woman I was drawn to it. I took it and placed it at my side.' His mother then tells him that the star and the axe signify 'a stout

man' whom he will meet; 'He is mightiest in the land; strength
he has.' This man, she says, he will love and in him acquire a
friend that will never forsake him.[1] These and numerous other
passages in the Gilgamesh poem seem to indicate that the friendship between Gilgamesh and Enkidu had an erotic aspect.

So far in this book I have concentrated on the homosexual
radical as it appears in dominance–submission relationships, and
its symbolic role has been the focus of interest. The story of
Enkidu and Gilgamesh exemplifies a union between grown men
of equal status, which is primarily erotic. Such relations, wherever
they occur, are always of a different character and fill a different
need from those hitherto dealt with (we are still discussing the
heterosexually potent male only).

The parallels in today's society are to be found in the kind of
relations referred to by Kinsey, existing between men living in
remote areas without access to women — 'lumbermen, cattlemen,
miners, hunters, and others engaged in out-of-door occupations'
— in whom neither personal nor social conflicts of any significance
arise out of this sexual activity (see Chapter 2, p. 52). Other contemporary examples would be the numerous homosexual liaisons
of heterosexual men in the Near East and North Africa.

Incidentally, it would be erroneous to believe that in such circumstances men imagine that their male sexual partner is a
woman. Regardless of whether these men would prefer women,
were they available, it is homosexual factors as such, the genitals
of the partner in particular, which are erotically stimulating. Men
seeking discharge of sexual tension with each other have turned
to a kind of relationship different from the heterosexual one, and
they are aroused by stimuli peculiar to that relation.

To the Norseman it was only the anal submission, the fact of
being *argr*, which was the cause of contempt. Phallic prowess over
other men was something to boast of openly. When one considers
these facts it is not at all unreasonable to suppose that genital relations existed among the Norsemen, and particularly among the

Vikings during their long voyages. (In passing, it is worth men-
tioning that homosexual relations among brothers-in-arms are
not at all rare; they are known, for example, among the North
American Indians and the New Caledonians.'[2]

The Norse blood-brother relationship naturally springs to
mind in this connection. In the saga of Gisli Sursson we have a
description of the solemn ritual of establishing blood-brother-
hood. A long strip of turf is cut in such a way that both ends remain fast in the ground. A spear, with runes cut in its shaft, is
used to lift the turf at the centre. The men crouch together beneath the turf, and each cuts a vein and lets the blood run into the
soil under the turf, mixing blood and soil. The blood-brothers
then kneel 'and swear to avenge each other, calling on the gods as
witness thereof'. The symbolism is clear; by going under the
turf which is fast to the ground they pass, as it were, through an
opening in the earth, thereby being reborn as brothers. Mixing
their blood in the soil makes them one in flesh and blood.

The more familiar one becomes with the attitudes and way of
life of these people, alien to our norms, prejudices and repressions
as they were, the more unlikely it seems that the blood-brother
relationship should not have included a genital aspect, based on
mutuality and equality between the partners. Glob has drawn
attention to the possibility that the blood-brother relationship may
be of very ancient origin in Denmark. He thinks it may have
existed among the 'Battle-Axe people' — that warlike equestrian
people who invaded Denmark from the South in about 2000 B.C.,
conquered the country and subdued the 'Megalithic' people who
were the rulers at that time. The 'Battle-Axe people' brought the
horse to Denmark and also a new burial custom, in which the dead
were buried either singly or in pairs. In the latter case, the 'double
graves' might contain a man and a woman or two men.[3] When
two men are buried in the same grave and in the same position as
man and woman this indicates, according to Glob, that these men
were blood-brothers.[4]

Such relationships, voluntarily established on the basis of equality, may well have been conflict-free, the equality serving to maintain undisturbed the dignity and self-esteem of both parties. However, in some cases it may have been difficult to preserve this equality. Aggressive tendencies, inherent in human nature, may have tempted one of the two to throw doubt on it, leading to alienation and tragedy, such as that in *The Blood-Brother's Saga* between Thorgeir and Thormód:

> Both Thorgeir and Thormód remained that summer at the Strands.* All men feared them and the strife they sowed around them like noxious weeds in a field. It is said that once at the height of their pride and insolence, Thorgeir said to Thormód: 'Do you know of any other man equal to us in keenness and manhood, and equally tested in deeds of valor?' Thormód replied: 'Men could surely be found who are no less brave than we.' Then Thorgeir said; 'And which of us would overcome the other if we two fought together?' Thormód answered: 'That I know not; but I know that this question of yours will put an end to our comradeship and fellowship and that we can no longer go along together.' Thorgeir said: 'I had not thought at all of trying to see who was the better man of us two.' Thormód replied, 'You were surely thinking of it while you spoke, and this will part our fellowship'. And this, indeed, was the outcome.[5]

The Thormód of the saga is the Thormód Kolbruneskald who fell at Stiklestad with his lord, Holy King Olaf. Long before that, however, he avenged the death of Thorgeir in fulfilment of their oath, in spite of their long separation from each other.

'Which of us would overcome the other if we fought together?' According to the attitudes of those times (compare the contest between Gudmund and Sinfjotli in Chapter 5), this question which Thorgeir put to Thormód might have been for-

* The name of a place.

mulated just as well in these words, 'Which of us, do you think, would be able to get the upper hand and make the other one *argr*?' Though the saga contains no indication of the existence of a sexual relationship between the two — possibly dropped during the process of retelling it and finally recording it in Christian times — there are still various leads in that direction. Neither of the two ever married. It is told unambiguously of Thorgeir that he 'cared little for women'. Thormód had a confused relationship with girls. On the one hand he sought their company — as we know from his famous poem in praise of a girl called Kolbrune — but the saga never relates that he had carnal knowledge of a woman. Rather, the opposite seems true; and certainly he was never able to tie himself to a woman, as he admits himself.

Thormód's love for King Olaf, whose man he was, was also deeper and more personal than was usual, I think, between house-carl and king or baron and prince, very close though these connections usually were. Before the battle of Stiklestad, Thormód, cast down by a premonition of misfortune, tried to console himself with the hope that they would fall together and that he and his king would end in the same place after death. He mourned when the king fell while he himself was still unharmed, and gladly welcomed the arrow which finally pierced his chest. Drawing it out and gazing at the shreds of his heart which clung to the barbs he praised the king one last time before falling to the ground, dead.

It is Thorgeir who reveals a conflict about his security in the brother relationship and Thormód who, sure of his power of judgment, draws the immediate conclusion that now they must part. It is not surprising that the conflict should lie with Thorgeir. From the description of their respective personalities Thormód is by far the wiser and more self-assured of the two.

It may be that the relationship between these two blood-brothers is different from the usual idea of sexual relationships between brothers-in-arms. The inhibited relations of both Thorgeir

and Thormód towards women could be an indication that
they were inverted homosexuals. In this case they come outside
the scope of this book. However that may be, the saga stresses
two things which are worth noting: firstly, how easily a conflict
of dominance–submission can well up between equals; and
secondly, how much the relationship between these men is taken
for granted in the saga, which casts no shadow of guilt or shame
upon them.

It is impossible to say whether a homosexually inverted personality structure formed the basis of all blood-brother relationships. It may not necessarily have been so at all, but the problem
of self-assertion is bound to have been somewhere near the surface,
and probably was the driving-force behind another blood-
brother tragedy, that of Gisli and Thorgrim in the saga of Gisli
Sursson.

In any case self-esteem is always vulnerable in sexual relations
between grown, virile men. What may happen if the self-respect
of one of the partners is hurt is strikingly exemplified in the following passage by Burton:

> During the years 1843–4 my regiment, almost all Hindu
> Sepoys of the Bombay Presidency, was stationed at a purga-
> tory called Bandar Ghárrá, a sandy flat with a scatter of
> verdigris-green milk-bush some forty miles north of Karáchi
> the headquarters. The dirty heap of mud-mat hovels, which
> represented the adjacent native village, could not supply a
> single woman; yet only one case of pederasty came to light
> and that after a tragical fashion some years afterwards. A
> young Brahman had connection with a soldier comrade of
> low caste and this had continued till, in an unhappy hour, the
> Pariah patient ventured to become the agent. The latter, in
> Arab: Al-fa'il – the 'doer' – is not an object of contempt like
> Al-Maful – the 'done'* – and the high-caste sepoy, stung by

* Notice the similarity between this attitude and that of the Norseman.

remorse and revenge, loaded his musket and deliberately shot his paramour. He was hanged by court martial at Hyderabad and, when his last wishes were asked, he begged in vain to be suspended by the feet; the idea being that his soul, polluted by exciting below the waist, would be doomed to endless trans-migrations through the lowest forms of life.[6]

Feelings of humiliation similar to those by which the higher ranking sepoy was seized, as the lower ranking soldier managed to mount him, are easily aroused between grown men. In the case of inverted homosexuals such conflicts probably partly explain why lasting, stable relationships are relatively rare between parties who are equal in age, quality of personality, and culture.

NOTES

1. J. B. Pritchard (Ed.), *Ancient Near Eastern Texts* (Princeton, New Jersey, 1955), p. 76 f.
2. Lafiteau, *Mœurs des sauvages américains*, and Foley, *Sur les habitations et les mœurs des Néo-Caledoniens*, quoted from Westermarck, *The Origin and Development of the Moral Ideas* (London, 1908), II, p. 457–60.
3. P. V. Glob, *Studie over den jyske enkeltgravskultur*, dissertation (Copenhagen, 1944), p. 179 ff.
4. P. V. Glob, *Danske Oldtidsminder* (Copenhagen, 1967), p. 81. An English translation, *Danish Prehistoric Monuments*, is in preparation by Faber and Faber (London).
5. *Fostbrødresagaen*. (An English translation is available: *Sagas of Kormak and of the Sworn-Brothers* [Princeton University Press, 1949].)
6. Richard Burton, *Thousand Nights and A Night*, Terminal Essay X (Benares, 1885), p. 237 f.

BOOK II

11

Rome before Christianity

In 120 B.C. Antinous, at twenty years of age, was drowned in the Nile, and became famous. He had been the beloved of Hadrianus, and the disconsolate emperor proclaimed his grief all over his realm. He had Antinous buried at the Porta Maggiore of Rome, and had numerous inscriptions made to commemorate him, while poets wrote poems of consolation to their mourning emperor;[1] he erected statues of the fair youth (Figure 17), and founded a city, Antinoopolis, at the place of the accident.

Hadrianus was one of the greatest emperors of Rome. He was a cosmopolitan of rare culture, travelled to all parts of his realm, was deeply absorbed in the culture of Egypt, and lived for a long time in Athens and the Greek cities of Asia Minor. He consorted with the best representatives of Greek learning, was initiated into the Eleusinian mysteries, and had a thorough knowledge of Greek art and antiquities. But first and foremost he was the emperor of Rome, the commander-in-chief of the army, sharing with it the hardships of camp life, and demanding of his soldiers strict discipline and great military skill. He had a correspondingly firm command of the administration, both financial and political. He watched steadily over Rome as well as over the provinces, and had the welfare of both equally at heart.[2]

This example of a relationship in late pre-Christian Hellenism shows, as did the life of the Greeks so many centuries earlier, that pederasty was not regarded as an abnormality, a kind of weakness

of the personality, in the way that we see it. Hadrianus was one
of the best men of his time, and his virility with women cannot
be called into question on the grounds of his relationship with
Antinous.

At the time of Hadrianus there lived in Delphi a man of noble
spirit and of social distinction: Plutarch. He was a priest at the
temple of Apollo, and it seems more than likely that he was one
of the learned Greeks with whom Hadrianus conversed. To
Plutarch we owe much of our knowledge of Dorian paiderasty.
His dialogue *Erotikós — A Dialogue on Love* — is of particular value,
because in it he quotes old sources otherwise lost. *Erotikós* is not
merely an archive, however; it supplies a wealth of lively description of the people of Plutarch's time, their points of view and
their attitudes to important aspects of life.

The dialogue is concerned with the question of whether it is in
a relationship with a man or a woman that a youth best learns the
nature of true love — that eros which elevates the soul and en-
nobles the personality. Sensuality is most explicitly distinguished
from eros. It is regarded as a matter of course by all the participants in the debate that a young man may satisfy his sensualism
with both sexes. What they disagree about so passionately is
whether the development of the *aretē* of a youth — the richest and
most beautiful blossoming of his virtue — is better furthered by an
erotic relationship with a man or a woman.[3]

Plutarch uses his son Autobulos as the narrator. The story runs
as follows; Ismenodora is a thirty-year-old widow of the city of
Thespiae in Boeotia. She is rich, of noble descent, and she leads a
blameless life even in her widowhood. Now she has fallen vio-
lently in love with Bacchon, a young man between eighteen and
twenty years of age, who is called 'The Handsome'. She has had a
series of meetings with him intending to arrange a marriage between him and a girl of her family. However, the impression he
has made on her, the many good things she has heard about him
and, furthermore, the sight of the many noble lovers (*erastai*)

crowding amorously around him, have moved her to want him for herself.[4] (Notice the difference from our world of thought; a woman finds her attraction to a young man strengthened by seeing him as the object of the amorous courtship of other men.)

Now a heated quarrel breaks out among the men surrounding Bacchon, all of them wanting the very best for him. Some strongly advocate marriage to Ismenodora, others are just as strongly against it. In order not to jeopardize their friendship the opposing parties agree to choose Plutarch as a mediator. Plutarch has just come to Thespiae together with his wife Timoxena whom he has recently married, to celebrate the Eros festival. His best friends are with him. At once they take part in the discourse, some of them being for the marriage, others against it.

The matter is further complicated by the fact that Bacchon's mother is worried by the splendour of Ismenodora's household. She is frightened by the thought that her beloved son might marry above his station. Furthermore his hunting companions depict marriage as a yoke. In his irresolution the young man leaves the decision to two of his older admirers who represent both sides. They in turn address themselves to Plutarch.

The arguments of both parties are based on the premise that true eros is smothered by violent sensual attraction. Love dies as soon as lust and enjoyment, unbridled carnal appetite and satisfaction become predominant in an erotic relationship. On this both parties agree. The one side, however, maintains that this applies to 'that lax and housebound love, that spends its time in the bosoms and beds of women';[5] true love has no more to do with women and girls than the love that flies feel for milk or bees for honey.[6] To make love to women is mere copulation, as is satisfying one's desire by using slave boys.[7] The other party argues just as strongly that nothing good ever comes of the love of boys, neither for the person who creeps stealthily into the *palaestra* to stare at the nakedness of young men, nor for those who caress and embrace and wait for the night when the guard is away.[8] Only

I

effeminacy and weakness are imparted to those 'who let themselves be covered and mounted like cattle'.⁹

Neither of the two parties deny man's sensuality, and that it may be directed as well towards one's own as towards the opposite sex. 'If then, Protogenus, we have regard for the truth, we will admit that the excitement we feel for boys or women is the same: it is Love';¹⁰ so one of the champions of marriage tells one of its opponents.

The idea is that sensual excitement should not be too great. It has to be tempered, otherwise eros, through which the personality develops towards *aretē*, cannot thrive. Each party claims that it is only possible in one way.

In view of the assumptions of our time, it is worth stressing that it is Ismenodora's strong, personal, passionate love of Bacchon which is the source of concern to those who are in opposition to his marrying her. The ordinary, conventionally arranged marriage which Ismenodora was in the process of bringing about with a girl of her kin would have caused no uproar.

Although Plutarch is expressly for marital love and is clearly siding with Ismenodora, he sets out both points of view in a formally impartial way as something on which good men hold different opinions. Neither does he let one of the parties gain victory over the other in the discussion. He puts an end to it by abruptly cutting the knot. Suddenly a horseman is sighted galloping towards them as though he brought news of war. He tells them that Ismenodora has taken the matter into her own hands by abducting the youth, and that she is now at her home preparing for the wedding. An appeal is made to the authorities, but as they themselves can come to no agreement, they refuse to interfere. In the end they all, reconciled, attend the wedding of Bacchon and Ismenodora.

Even though the temple of Apollo at Delphi was still held in high esteem at the time of Plutarch, he was conscious of living in the afterglow of Greece's glory. So he looked back to the times of his country's greatness, thus leaving to the world much information about that epoch from sources lost to us. Conceivably, then, the *Dialogue on Love* might be thought to be an imitation antique, made after the pattern of Plato. If this were the case, then the arguments of the pro-pederasty party could be a purely literary artefact, lacking genuine roots in Plutarch's own time. The relationship of Hadrianus to Antinous and the respect shown it by the contemporary world is one of the proofs that this was not so. *Erotikós* deals with the living reality of its own time.

These two examples — Hadrianus' love of Antinous and Plutarch's story — show both how close, and also how remote, ancient Hellas was to late pre-Christian Hellenism. Pederasty as an erotic phenomenon, elaborated aesthetically and ethically, still existed as something belonging naturally to life as in the Athens of Socrates more than five hundred years earlier. But the difference stands out by comparison with the paiderasty of ancient Sparta. To Hadrianus the relationship with Antinous was a personal matter, respected by the society in which he lived in the same way as other serious emotional relations. But whatever ethical and aesthetic component there was in the relationship was an individual and private matter between the two. Pederasty was no longer a means employed by the state in the education of the young, controlled by its highest authorities and an obligation for the best men to take upon themselves. It was not institutionalized any longer, had no place in the cult, and its symbols had ceased to be the generally recognized expressions of the noblest aims of the communal life of the society. These symbols were no longer active in general in the service of The Good Life — that manner of life which serious men strove to attain. In the late Hellenistic period pederasty is to be regarded primarily as an erotic phenomenon.

And as pure erotism, homosexuality was a prominent element in pre-Christian Hellenism. A vast homosexual prostitution existed — on the whole, as in former times, there were no moralistic attitudes towards prostitution—and in his *Satyricon*, Petronius, Nero's elegant *maître de plaisir*, depicts the sexual abandon of his characters as a pell-mell of shared hetero- and homosexual relations. The same attitude is found in the works of Catullus, Tibullus, Vergil, and many others, and, to the extent that Suetonius may be relied upon, we can believe that homosexuality formed part, too, of the erotic many-sidedness of Nero and Caligula.

In the state religion of Rome phallic worship did not occupy any important place. The phallus seems to have appeared in only one important context in the cult. *Mutinus Titinus* was a stone phallus which was used at the weddings of the most outstanding patricians in the earliest times. The ceremony, named *confarreatio*, was performed in the presence of the *Pontifex Maximus* or the *Flamen Dialis* (the highest priest of Jove) and ten witnesses. In later times this type of wedding ceremony became exceedingly rare, probably because divorce was very difficult to obtain if the wedding had been performed by *confarreatio*. During the ceremony certain sacrifices were performed, and then the bride sat down upon *Mutinus Titinus*, thereby deflowering herself. Except for this very rare ceremony there were no phallic rites that we know of in the official religion of Rome.

However, Priapus appears, in local belief, often in a humorous context. He was sometimes placed in orchards where his huge phallus, painted red, would frighten birds and thieves away—see for instance Horatius, *Satire* I, VIII. Then, too, Ovid tells us of the humorous reason for the incessant erection of Priapus. While he was courting a nymph and when she was on the point of giving in to him, she was frightened by the sudden braying of a donkey nearby and ran away, leaving him behind with an ever-persistent erection. (*Fasti* I, 391 ff.)

Images of phalli were common everywhere—they can still be seen in Pompeii.

Augustus demonstrates the striking difference between the attitude of the Romans and our own attitude to the male genital. Horatius, whom he valued highly, he jokingly calls his *purissimum penem* — 'my very best penis'.[11] The genital was still no *pudendum*, nothing to be ashamed of.

NOTES

1. Pauly-Wissowa, *Realencyclopädie*, s.v. Antinoos and Antinoopolis.
2. See for instance M. Rostovtzeff, *Rome* (New York, 1960), p. 209.
3. Plutarch, The Dialogue on Love, *Moralia* 750.
4. Op. cit. 749 D.
5. Op. cit. 751 B.
6. Op. cit. 750 C.
7. Op. cit. 751 B.
8. Op. cit. 751 F–752 A.
9. Op. cit. 751 E.
10. Op. cit. 751 F.
11. Suetonius, *The Twelve Caesars*.

12

The Chosen People

And the sight of the glory of the Lord was like devouring fire on the top of the mount in the eyes of the children of Israel. And Moses went into the midst of the cloud, and gat him up into the mount: and Moses was in the mount forty days and forty nights.[1]

And the Lord said unto Moses, 'Go, get thee down; for thy people, which thou broughtest out of the land of Egypt, have corrupted themselves: they have turned aside quickly out of the way which I commanded them: they have made them a molten (golden) calf, and have worshipped it, and have sacrificed thereunto, and said, These be thy gods, O Israel, which have brought thee up out of the land of Egypt.'[2]

And Moses turned, and went down from the mount, and the two tables of the testimony were in his hand.[3]

And it came to pass, as soon as he came nigh unto the camp, that he saw the calf, and the dancing: and Moses' anger waxed hot, and he cast the tables out of his hands, and brake them beneath the mount.[4]

The Lord said, 'Neither shalt thou go up by steps unto mine altar, that thy nakedness be not discovered thereon'.[5]

The Lord said, 'And thou shalt make them (the priests) linen breeches to cover their nakedness; from the loins even unto the thighs they shall reach.'[6]

The Lord said, 'And if any man's seed of copulation go out
from him, then he shall wash all his flesh in water, and be
unclean until the even. And every garment, and every skin,
whereon is seed of copulation, shall be washed with water,
and be unclean until the even.[7]

'I am the Lord. Thou shalt not lie with mankind, as with
womankind: it is abomination. And whosoever shall commit any such abomination shall be cut off from among their
people.'[8]

These significant quotations from the Old testament show
clearly how exceptional were the Jews among the other cultures
of the Mediterranean and the Near East. Unlike classical Greece,
pre-Christian Rome, Egypt, and many other cultures, Israel condemned phallic worship (the molten calf—Baal, a bull god—was
a phallic god, of course); the homosexual relationship was an
abomination, punishable by death; the genital a *pudendum*, something shameful, and the seed was unclean.

The difference between the Jew and the Greek is exposed in
the comparison of the Old Testament Hebrew word for the
male genital with the Greek one used in the sixth song of the
Odyssey. Here is an account of what happened when Odysseus
was thrown up naked on the shores of Phaeacia and met Nausicaa,
daughter of the Phaeacian king. Before appearing before her from
his hiding place in the bushes 'he broke with his stout hand from
the thick wood a leafy branch, that he might hold it about him
and hide therewith his nakedness.'[9] The Greek word for genital
used here—*mēdea*—is a neutral word without a connotation of
shame or the like. Odysseus is not ashamed in our sense because
of his naked genital. He covers his nakedness because it is not
appropriate for a man of his standing to appear without garments
in a situation of this kind. Correspondingly, on the many Attic
vases showing the god Dionysus surrounded by naked, phallic
satyrs, he always appears in a long garment (Figure 19); so in

spite of his surname *Phalēs* he is never represented as visibly phallic. The long garment of the god is a sign of dignity, in fact, not a cover of nakedness. It is obvious that no question of pudicity was involved in the case of Odysseus and Nausicaa since, had Odysseus been a participant in the Olympian Games, Nausicaa, an unmarried girl, might freely have witnessed his performance[10] which took place in complete nakedness. Married women were forbidden to be present as onlookers on pain of death.[11] However, since this prohibition did not extend to unmarried girls it is hardly likely that it had anything to do with pudicity between the sexes. The reason for it is unknown.

There is another situation, equally serious and of a primarily asexual nature, in which Odysseus might have appeared with naked *mēdea* in the presence of women, and that is when he was armed for battle, like Achilles in the Attic vase-painting (Figure 18).

The Hebrew word, *ērva*, has a sexual connotation, meaning shameful, hideous flesh, flesh which has to be covered.

Philology here shows how different were the views of the Greeks and the Jews: the Greeks regarded the phallus and paiderasty as sacred and the seed as the carrier of *aretē*, while the Jews saw homosexuality as an abomination, the phallus as hideous and seed as unclean.

In passing it may be noted that the laws of Moses did not forbid sexual relations between women. To the Jews, as to most other people, it was of no interest what women did among themselves.

The Jews had not always lived according to the Mosaic laws. The latter apply only to the period after the Babylonian exile, that is after *c.* 600 B.C. Before that time phallic worship formed part of the cult, and male homosexual prostitution existed in the royal temple of Jerusalem. These prostitutes were known as *quādēs*, 'Sacred Men', and had their official rooms in the temple.[12] Intercourse with these men was a sacred act, paid for by a fee to the temple.

Neither had the typical attitude to the naked genital developed at that time: David was seen dancing 'with all his might ... uncovering himself' before the Ark of the Lord.[13]

After the return of the Jews from exile, a number of radical reforms were instigated by which the Jewish cult was purged of sexual elements of Canaanite origin. From then on, the condemnation of everything phallic and of homosexuality was an important sign of Jewish orthodoxy.

As we know, this small, gifted, self-assertive and militant people exerted a great influence on European history and culture, not least in their condemnation of phallic symbolism. Through the spread of Judeo-Christian communities throughout the Roman empire, Jewish influence began to be felt even before Hadrianus exiled the Jews in A.D. 135. This was the outcome of the last Jewish revolt against the Romans led by Simon Bar Kochba. Having finally defeated the Jews after long and fierce fighting, and not without a great deal of trouble, Hadrianus expelled them from their country, and they dispersed to every corner of the empire.

NOTES

1. Exodus XXIV, 17–18.
2. Op. cit. XXXII, 7–8.
3. Op. cit. XXXII, 15.
4. Op. cit. XXXIII, 19–20.
5. Op. cit. XX, 26.
6. Op. cit. XXVIII, 42.
7. Leviticus XV, 16–18.
8. Op. cit. XVIII, 22.
9. The *Odyssey*, song 6, lines 117–29.
10. Pausanias, VI, 20, 9.
11. Op. Cit., V, 6, 7.
12. Joh. Pedersen, *Israel*, (Copenhagen and London, 1940), IV
    pp. 470–71.
13. 2 Samuel VI, 14–23.

13

The Advent of Christianity

For this cause God gave them up unto vile affections: for even their women did change the natural use into that which is against nature: And likewise also the men, leaving the natural use of the woman, burned in their lust one toward another; men with men working that which is unseemly, and receiving in themselves that recompense of their error which was meet ... Who knowing the judgment of God, that they which commit such things are worthy of death, not only do the same, but have pleasure in them that do them.[1]*

Thus speaks St Paul, the temperamental apostle of Christ, in his letter to the Romans. He speaks of the heathen, but actually it seems as if a warning to the Christian Romans is implicit in what he says, just as his well-founded words to the Corinthians indicate that not everything with them was proper by the standards of the righteous Jew.[2] And this is by no means strange. Paul's mission was in a Greco-Roman world completely lacking the Jewish view of sexual acts and symbols. This absence of prejudice may even have weakened the morals of the immigrant Jews. Besides, the congregations to whom he addressed himself comprised not only Jews but, as he expressly states, Greeks and Bar-

---

* It is a remarkable sign of the zeal of St Paul that he even paid attention to homosexual acts among women.

barians as well, and to these the Jewish attitude was quite alien. Conceivably Paul had not only ordinary immorality to fight within the congregations, but quite un-Jewish sexual elements, which may even have been part of the practice of their cult.

Jewish morality was victorious. At the Council of Elvira in A.D. 300, it was decreed that last rites should be denied to those who had used boys for the satisfaction of their lust. And the Christian Church, given legal status by the Emperor Constantine, and made the one and only Church by his successors, was dominated entirely by the sexual morality of the laws of Moses.

This had the most drastic effect on the Roman Empire. As an immediate consequence of the elevation of Christianity to the status of a state religion the secular penal code was brought into conformity with the laws of the Old Testament. So during the fourth century A.D., homosexuality was made a capital crime, to be punished by the sword according to Theodosius and by burning according to Valentinian. A veritable crusade against homosexuality followed.[3]

It is not difficult to imagine the shocking effect of this on populations to whom traditionally homosexuality, and pederasty in particular, had been regarded as a matter of course, in no way to be morally condemned, and even, in some circumstances, to be regarded with respect. Remember that the victory of Christianity over heathenism took place only two hundred years after the time of Hadrianus and Antinous. But once Christianity gained supremacy, homosexuality—sodomy—became tantamount to religious infidelity, and the wages of this sin were death.

During the first centuries of Christianity the situation was not eased—on the contrary. In the sixth century A.D. the emperor Justinian proceeded against 'unnatural lust' still more harshly. He had been shaken by the catastrophes which had befallen his realm —famine, earthquake and plague—and he gave these as reasons for his severe anti-homosexual measures; they were necessary lest such acts of desecration cause whole cities to perish, and the inhabitants with them, as had happened before, according to the Holy Scripture.[4]

Gibbon deals with this subject in the following words: 'I touch with reluctance, and dispatch with impatience a more odious vice, of which modesty rejects the name, and nature abominates the idea.'[5] Obviously Gibbon saw nothing good in homosexuality, but Justinian's harshness he finds difficult to justify:

> [Justinian] declared himself the implacable enemy of unmanly lust, and the cruelty of his persecutions can scarcely be excused by the purity of his motives. In defiance of every principle of justice, he stretched to past as well as future offences the operations of his edicts, with the previous allowance of a short respite for confession and pardon. A painful death was inflicted by the amputation of the sinful instrument, or the insertion of sharp reeds into the pores and tubes of most exquisite sensibility; and Justinian defended the propriety of the execution, since the criminals would have lost their hands had they been convicted of sacrilege. In this state of disgrace and agony two bishops, Isaiah of Rhodes and Alexander of Diospolis, were dragged through the streets of Constantinople, while their brethren were admonished by the voice of a crier to observe this awful lesson, and not to pollute the sanctity of their character. Perhaps these prelates were innocent ... A sentence of death and infamy was often founded on the slight and suspicious evidence of a child or a servant, and pederasty became the crime of those to whom no crime could be imputed.[6]

Thus what was originally an exclusively Jewish attitude towards homosexuality and phallic symbolism had gained ascendancy over the whole Christian world. A true Christian believer was marked out, from then on, by his unconditional condemnation of everything homosexual. Correspondingly, homosexual acts

were regarded as unshakeable proof of heterodoxy. In this respect
we were all turned into Jews before the Lord.

Thus the early Church established the official Christian attitude
towards homosexuality and phallic symbolism for ever after. It
seems, however, that in the course of time the Church's approach
to sodomy changed. Of course sodomy continued to be a sin
demanding confession and penance. However, it seems that the
Roman Church of the Middle Ages did not deliver up the sinner
to the severe punishment of the secular arm. And homosexuality
per se was no longer considered a basis for an accusation of heresy.
However, if the primary accusation was one of heresy, charges
of sodomy followed inevitably, often not unfounded, as will be
shown later, in Chapter 15. It is against this background that we
should consider the dictum of St Thomas Aquinas that unnatural
intercourse is a sin even more detestable than incest and fornica-
tion.[7] At the time of Thomas, in the thirteenth century, the
Church of Rome felt profoundly threatened by the Cathars, a
powerful heretical movement in southern France, which the
Church finally managed to have exterminated by a veritable crusade, led by the French king and aided by the Germans. The
Cathars were held to be sodomites, which accounts for the strong
words of Thomas. It is doubtful whether he was much concerned
with what took place among good orthodox farm-hands and
farm-boys, or between counts, barons and pages for that matter.

The attitude of the Church to homosexuality during the
Middle Ages may be regarded as determined by its relationship
to heretics—just as its stand on phallic worship in the sixteenth
and seventeenth centuries was affected by the fight against witch-
craft.

NOTES

1. Romans I, 26 ff.
2. 1 Corinthians VI.
3. Quoted from E. Westermarck, *The Origin and Development of the Moral Ideas* (London, 1908), II, p. 480 ff.
4. Westermarck, op. cit.
5. Edward Gibbon, *The History of the Decline and Fall of the Roman Empire* (London, 1854), V, p. 321. (The first edition of Gibbon's work was 1776–88.)
6. Gibbon, op. cit., p. 323.
7. Thomas Aquinas, *Summa Theologica* II–II, 154, 12.

14

Christian Denmark in the Twelfth Century

One of the best of Denmark's Romanesque village churches, rich in fine granite sculpture, is situated at Tømmerby in northern Jutland. In a corner of the porch stands an impressive granite phallus 130 cm (4 feet 3 inches) high (Figure 20). It is Romanesque, made in the twelfth century, about two hundred years after the adoption of Christianity by the Danes. As a representation of a phallus it is an extraordinary synthesis of naturalism and stylization. The proportions are true to nature. The head — *glans* — is quite naturalistic, dome-shaped and with an opening at the top. The lower border of the head — *corona glandis* — is clearly set off in a finely stylized manner. The upper part of the shaft is cylindrical, the lower part octagonal with Romanesque ornamentation — tracery and spirals — on some of the facets, and on one of them (to be seen in the middle of the picture), a cross. According to reports in the files of the National Museum in Copenhagen, in earlier times this phallus stood at one side of the church door — one is tempted to say like the *herma* at a Greek temple. In 1810 it was found built into the wall of the porch; later it was removed and in 1934 it was placed behind the apse (see Figure 21). Later again it was moved to its present site in the south-east corner of the porch. It is probable that originally it was a tombstone, as were many *bauta*-stones of former times. Miraculously it escaped being destroyed, and there it stands now, placed by sensible people in the antechamber to God's house as a living reminder, telling us that our forefathers brought central parts of their old cult into the new one, holding for a long time to the sacred images and vital symbols of their fathers. There is nothing primitive about the phallus of Tømmerby. It is a noble piece of Romanesque sculpture, and it carries the token of the Church: the Cross. It was not unique in its time in Denmark. On the sides of some of the Romanesque baptismal fonts sculptors carved phallic figures similar to the Frey figures of pre-Christian times. Thus two hundred years after the coming of Christianity to Denmark the phallic symbol still found its place even on the vessel of baptism, which gave access to the community of the church. And the twelfth century was the period of the finest flowering of the Danish Church, when stone churches were arising throughout the country showing how both nobles and commoners were gathering around the cult of Christ, eager to make their contribution to it. It might seem strange that at this time such unmistakeable signs of the survival of the old heathen phallic worship, sanctified by the presence of the Cross, could be found in the Church. To understand this, it is necessary to remember the way in which Christianity came to Denmark. It came late and peacefully, in the tenth century, and was adopted voluntarily by king and people at the *Things* (the general assemblies).

To people like the Danes at that time the changing from one religion to another was different from our notion of conversion. To us, conversion means primarily the act of renouncing a false belief or disbelief—an illusion or a false conviction, the unreality of which one is led to understand—in favour of the right belief in something which is considered true and real.

It was not so with the Danes. They did not suddenly discover that the gods they had worshipped from ancient times had never existed in reality. They turned away from their old gods, withdrawing their loyalty, as they might from a king or earl, in favour of another god who, they had been convinced, was stronger and thus more worth their while to follow. They deprived their old gods of sacrifice and cult, knowing they would lose their power. The gods did not disappear, they just became weak and evil.

Christ, to whom they transferred their cult, was for a long time conceived in the image of Odin, Thor or Frey, who had been the main gods hitherto. They saw Christ as a great king or chieftain, full of power, good fortune—*spéd*, as it would be called in Anglo-Saxon—and generosity.

The old festivals and cultic customs had a power of survival by which many of them were perpetuated within the new creed or outside it. In this respect Rome always displayed flexibility and tactical wisdom. In Imperial Rome of the late pre-Christian period the state religion adopted the worship of *sol invictus*—the unconquered sun. *Sol invictus* was connected with several of the rival religions of that time. Baal, Mithras and Apollo as well as Mars were identified with it. A special cult was established, an ostentatious temple built, and its supreme priest became a member of the pontifical college.[1] The main festival of this cult was held on December 25th, *dies natalis solis invicti*—'the birthday of the unconquered sun'. When Christianity became the state religion and all rival creeds were forbidden, the Church adopted this day of celebration as one of the cornerstones of the ecclesiastical year, making it the birthday of Christ. In this way, an important festival had been taken over from earlier cults; and a more fitting surname for the resurrected Redeemer than 'the unconquered' could hardly be found. In the case of the voluntary adoption of Christianity by an independent people against whom it was not possible to employ force, the Church of Rome would be willing to show a similar, or even a greater flexibility.

The greatest heathen festival of the North, *Yule*, only had to be moved slightly in time. In Denmark, *Yule* fell around February 1st. So to make it coincide with the festival of Christ's birth it simply had to be pulled back a few weeks to the time of the winter

K

solstice. The result is that Christmas in Scandinavia remains the most important festival of the year, retaining a significance never acquired by Easter, though from a Christian point of view the festival of the Passion and the Resurrection is far more important. Here is a great difference between Scandinavia and the southern countries which were Christianized much earlier.

In the North, the ritual slaughtering of sacrificial animals was not taken over by the cult of Christ. The paschal lamb did not take the place of the old sacrificial animals as it did in Greece. The *Yule* slaughtering at Yuletide was detached from the ecclesiastical cult. It remained, however, even until close to our own time as a ritual act charged with ancient symbolism more or less clearly apprehended. As recently as the end of the last century it was still an important ritual in which ancient customs and beliefs existed independently of the Church. The slaughtering had to take place at the right time of year and at a certain hour, in many places before sunrise. The animal was shown the same consideration and respect as at a sacrifice; certain formulas were addressed to it, assurances that it was not being killed out of hate. The knife was blessed, and it was considered important that the animal be given a good death—nobody was allowed to show it pity; that would make death hard for it. The blood had to stream freely into the vessel and clot properly when stirred[2]—just as had been done a thousand years earlier at the Norse *Yule* sacrifice.[3] And the black-pudding sausages, made everywhere in Denmark until the beginning of this century, were more than mere food.

In the 1880s, on a farm* in the extreme north-west of Jutland, the far-reaching importance of these black-pudding sausages was suddenly and strikingly revealed. The farmer's wife had been converted to the sectarian belief of a Norwegian woman missionary who had made an impact at the time in that part of the country. The farmer, some twenty years older than his wife and untouched by the evangelizing power of the missionary, accepted

* Named *Vanggaard*.

the situation patiently, until his wife, convinced by the missionary's righteous belief in the decrees of the Old Testament, ventured to demand that they forgo the black-pudding sausages and that the blood be thrown away after the slaughtering. Blood and intestines were unclean and forbidden according to Holy Scripture. However, there she went too far. The farmer and his foreman were so insistent on their continuing with the custom of sausage-making that she had to give way. The pig was strung up by its hind feet and its neck arteries were slit in the proper manner. Just as the blood was streaming into the vessel and being stirred, the pig suddenly vomited a large part of the contents of its stomach into the blood, thus making it useless. Instantly the farmer and his foreman realized that a sign had been given them. The sausages were banned. Heathenism had finally been expelled from the farm.

Considering that the *Yule* festival, the slaughtering ritual, the drinking of toasts, and other heathen customs were such diehards, it is not surprising that a powerful symbol like the phallus and the cult surrounding it could not be eradicated immediately on the adoption of Christianity in Denmark. For a considerable period it had to be tolerated within the new cult, alien to it though it was. However, from the twelfth century onwards I know of no signs of open, unveiled phallic worship within the Church.

NOTES

1. Kurt Latte, *Römische Religionsgeschichte* (Munich, 1960), p. 349.
2. A. Olrik and H. Ellekilde, *Nordens Gudeverden* (*The Gods of the North*), (Copenhagen, 1951), II, p. 911 ff.
3. Vilhelm Grønbech, *The Culture of the Teutons* (London and Copenhagen, 1925), p. 260 ff.

15

The Heretics

In the beginning was the Word [*Logos*], and the Word was with God, and the Word was God ... In him was life; and the life was the light of men. And the light shineth in darkness; and the darkness overcame it not ... And the world knew him not ... And the Word was made flesh, and dwelt among us (and we beheld his glory, the glory as of the only begotten of the Father), full of grace and truth.

These words, taken from the prologue of the Gospel according to St John, precisely express the ideas which are central to a number of religious views emerging around the time of the birth of Christ—in Palestine as well as elsewhere, as we know from the Dead Sea Scrolls. Differing in detail from place to place, these religious movements, regarded as varieties of Gnosticism, were united by two main features: they were dualistic, and they maintained that *gnōsis*—that is, knowledge of God acquired through a direct personal experience of His presence—was the only true basis of a religious life. Belief—*pistis*—was not enough in itself.

The different Gnostic movements grew during the first three centuries A.D., and throughout the next thousand years they were to prove a menace to the supremacy of the Church of Rome, compelling her at times to fight for her life. In this book I shall be dealing with the Hellenistic Gnostics and their medieval successors because of their particular attitude towards homosexuality and the effect it had on the Church.

Dualism was the word used to describe the chasm between God and the world, light and darkness, spirit and body, good and evil, life and death. God was so entirely outside this world that the world had no knowledge of Him at all. He was called 'the alien', or 'the unknown God', and it was said that 'the world knew him not'. He had had nothing to do with the creation of the world — the 'demiurge', identified with Jahve or Satan, was responsible for that. God was light, spirit, goodness and life. The world, matter, the body was darkness and death. However, a spark of the divine light had fallen into each body, and, glowing there in its dark prison, this spark was ever longing to be reunited with the divine light, to be one with it again — 'to be with God, to be God'. And God then sent a part of Himself, His son Jesus, down to earth to show the many divine sparks the way back to Him.

The light, the spirit, cannot be conquered by the darkness, the body — 'the light shineth in the darkness, and the darkness overcame it not'. The darkness of the body cannot extinguish the divine sparks of the spirit, but it can keep them prisoner and hinder their reunion with the great light. However, if mankind understands and follows the teaching of Jesus, as interpreted by the Gnostics, then the light of the spirit may conquer the darkness and free itself from the body and its constraints.

It followed on directly from the teaching of the Gnostics that everything serving physical reproduction had to be evil. They were fanatical adversaries of procreation. By begetting children you merely created new body prisons for divine sparks. According to the Gnostics it was better for mankind to commit suicide, if by no other method then by putting an end to all procreation.

So the Gnostics sought redemption from this world in two ways: through *gnōsis* and through delivery from the flesh.

Gnōsis is a word which can be traced back to Plato — although he preferred the words *epistēmē* or *theōria* — means direct knowledge of God, the beholding of the divine light. This does not mean intellectual understanding. The word *gnōsis* refers to an experience which is direct and personal — in short a mystical experience such as was described by Plato in the *Symposium*[1] or by the mystics of India, by Bernard of Clairvaux — the embittered enemy of the medieval Gnostics — by Meister Eckhart and many others.

The way in which 'mystic' is used in everyday language implies something which is obscure, incomprehensible and conceptually confused. However, it should be remembered that to persons who have had mystical experiences it means something quite different. To them the mystical state is clear, concrete, tangible, real, containing nothing confused or inconceivable. However, it is difficult, in fact well-nigh impossible, to describe these experiences in our language, which is primarily directed towards the communication of things and situations perceived by our ordinary sense organs; the mystical experience, however real to the person who has it, is not perceived through the organs of sense. Nowadays a number of people have had experiences more or less similar to mystical ones through the effects of the drug LSD. Besides, a number of 'ordinary' people experience mystical states; but, knowing that they would never be able to convey an understanding of them to other people, they usually keep them to themselves.

It is common for mystics to describe their experience as a confrontation with something transcendental; they say they have the sensation of becoming one with this phenomenon which belongs outside the world of the senses and which many find it natural to call God. Often it is accompanied by an experience of seeing light. While this 'being-with-God-being-God' experience takes possession of a person, all feelings related to the body and its needs and cravings disappear. For the Gnostics this was the natural foundation of their belief in the dualistic division between spirit and matter.

Although they were against procreation, contrary to many other mystics most Gnostics did not find abstinence as such valuable. The reverse, indeed, was sometimes true. While some regarded the body with indifference, others felt an obligation to do everything for the satisfaction of the body which had been forbidden by the Church of Rome. From this latter attitude sprang what has been called Gnostic libertinism.

Those Gnostics who were indifferent to the body held that the chasm between the divine spark and the body was such that the body and its doings could exert no influence on the divine light of the spirit. Whatever the body did was unimportant, provided it abstained from action resulting in procreation. So they had nothing against infertile heterosexual or homosexual relationships or against other 'unnatural' forms of sexual satisfaction. Rather, they held the view, parallel to that of St Paul, that it was better to provide for the satisfaction of the flesh than to be disturbed by a burning dissatisfaction.

The Gnostics who held the other point of view, that carnal activity should be encouraged, felt that just as 'the hidden God', whom 'the world knew not', had nothing to do with the material world, so He had no part in the laws and rules governing human conduct in this world. All that was the work of the demiurge, Jahve, and one had to free oneself of his moral laws by transgressing them all. To fall short of that goal in this life meant that one would be sent back after death in a new incarnation to make good the omission.[2]

However, an alternative to this libertinism existed in many Gnostic sects. Despite the apparent contradiction, the same dualistic doctrine provided a basis for the strictest abstinence and asceticism. It was practised by a nucleus of the highest within each sect, 'the pure', 'the perfect', 'the chosen' who possessed the true *gnōsis*. It was felt that the 'believers' surrounding this group,

having only *pistis*—belief—could not and should not live
abstinently.

The freedom, even encouragement, to indulge in all manner
of 'unnatural' sexual practices, including homosexuality, became
one of the greatest stumbling-blocks in the eyes of the Church.
The Gnostics' many deviations from the law of the Old Testament confirmed the Church in its old idea that heresy and
sodomy were inextricably intertwined.

Replete with heresies Gnosticism certainly was. Firstly, in its
idea of the dualism of spirit and body. Though St Paul was as
firm a dualist as any Gnostic he did not manage to affect the attitude of the Church on this point. The Church was monistic, as
was clearly expressed in, for instance, its concepts of death and
resurrection; the dead slept in their bodies until on Doomsday
they rose in full carnality. (Consequently the medieval apparition
of the dead was solid and corporeal, not an airy ghost that one
could walk through.) Clearly, the anti-social views held by the
Gnostics on marriage, procreation and ownership were incompatible, too, with those of a Church supported by the secular
state. Furthermore the Gnostics hated the Cross as the instrument
of Jesus's torture. They reduced the Holy Virgin's status to that
of a mere channel giving passage to Jesus. In addition, many of
them refused to admit that Jesus had possessed a body of His own
in the true sense. That part of Himself which the hidden God sent
down to the world as His son chose at random, so they believed,
the body of some earthly man as His dwelling. The moving words
on the cross, 'My God, my God, why hast Thou forsaken me?',
difficult of interpretation as they are, would then be the despairing
cry of this poor carnal man after the spirit of Jesus had left him
to be reunited with his Father. For this reason the words of St
John, 'And the Word was made flesh', became an issue between
the Church and the Gnostics.

One of the most eminent of Gnostics was Mani, born A.D.
216, who worked in Persia, called himself the Apostle of Jesus

Christ, and ended by being crucified. His dualistic teachings, Manichaeism, acquired an immense importance. Throughout the Hellenistic period and the Middle Ages it spread to Egypt, through Asia Minor, via Constantinople to the Balkans, and Bulgaria in particular. From there it was carried to northern Italy and southern France. The names by which the adherents of Manichaeism called themselves changed from place to place: Barbēlo-Gnostics, Paulicians, Patarenes, Bogomiles and Cathars—but Manichaean they were and remained. In Bulgaria the movement, supported by the king and the nobility, played an enormous role far into the Middle Ages and became a great problem to the Papal Church. The reputation of the Manichees for practising homosexuality remained unchanged throughout the centuries. A thousand years after the time of Mani, when Manichaeism had spread from Bulgaria to southern France, one of the names given to its adherents there was 'Bulgarian', in French 'Bougre', transformed in English to 'Bugger'—to this day the word for a sodomite.

In southern France Manichaeism became firmly rooted. Its adherents were called Albigensians—the city of Albi was one of their main centres—or Cathars, meaning 'the pure'. (The Danish word for a heretic, *kaetter*, is derived from Cathar.) From the eleventh to the thirteenth century the whole of southern France was dominated by the Cathars who won over by their puritanism not only the common people but also the more influential burghers and, most important of all, the nobility. They were supported openly by the counts of Toulouse, Foix and Bézier and the king of Aragonia. The central group, 'the chosen', 'the pure', or 'the perfect', lived a life of asceticism, the purity of which was admitted even by their enemy, Bernard of Clairvaux. But the 'believers' were subject to no such restrictions, and there were reasons enough for the accusations of immorality in general and sodomy in particular made by the horrified Church. This was undoubtedly the background against which St Thomas Aquinas framed his pronouncement that sodomy was an even graver sin than incest.*

The Cathars believed neither in hell nor in purgatory. They distrusted the Old Testament. The Gospel according to St John was the most holy scripture to them, its prologue in particular. They opposed and despised the Church. The princes and the most powerful of the nobles seized the property of the Church backed by the religious authority of the Cathars.

Finally the Pope succeeded in persuading the French king to undertake a virtual crusade against the Cathars. It was carried through by the aid of Germans, eager to participate in the looting of the rich lands of southern France. The war lasted for most of the first half of the thirteenth century. It was cruel in the extreme – the pyres of the Inquisition flamed everywhere – and it led to the total eradication of the Cathar movement. The last fight took place at Monségur, a nearly impregnable castle, for a long time the main establishment of the Cathars, which had been presented to them by the Count of Foix. Hopelessly outnumbered, the Cathars could not hold the fortress for ever. When the end seemed near, the greater part of the defenders received the *Consolamentum*, the final rite bestowing 'perfection', although by doing so they condemned themselves to the fires of the Inquisition. After the surrender of Montségur the 'perfect', about two hundred, were burnt without trial.[3]

As a point of ecclesiastical politics, it is interesting that, in the same way that the ancient Church annexed the birthday of the unconquered sun, December 25th, the medieval Church made more and more use of the prologue of the Gospel according to St John. At first it was kept as the text of the sermon given on December 25th. However, in certain places in the eleventh and

---

* Curiously enough there is support for this thesis in Genesis XIX, 30–38. Following immediately upon the story of Sodom's sin and punishment comes that of the incest between the daughters of Lot and their father, whom they had first made drunk. This does not result in any punishment. On the contrary, the two daughters provide the line of descent of two mighty peoples, the Moabites and the Ammonites.

twelfth centuries it began to be recited by the priest on his way back from the altar after Mass; at some unknown date but certainly before the end of the thirteenth century it had become a general custom, although it was not made obligatory by decree till 1570.[4] The Catholic interpretation of the words 'And the Word was made flesh' was underlined by a genuflection.

Simultaneously with the spreading use of the prologue of St John came the introduction of light into the Church. The house of God was transformed into a palace of light. It was Suger, the abbot of St Denis, the ecclesiastical centre of the French monarchy, who introduced the Gothic style into church architecture. According to Otto von Simson the most important characteristic of the Gothic style is neither the pointed arch nor the ribbed vault, but the glass walls which Suger substituted for the solid walls of the Romanesque church. He built the choir of St Denis with walls consisting of extensive stained glass windows separated by stone frames. This choir became the model for the cathedrals of Chartres, Notre Dame, Canterbury and all later genuine Gothic churches. Suger's introduction of the worship of light is explained by von Simson as follows: the patron saint of France, St Denis, was identified at that time with Pseudo-Dionysius, a neo-platonic mystic, who lived in Syria towards the end of the fifth century A.D. He in turn was confused with the Dionysius mentioned in the Acts[5] as being a disciple of St Paul, an Athenian of distinction, and a member of the Areopagus Council. Because of the latter confusion a degree of holiness was ascribed to the books of Pseudo-Dionysius which elevated them to a status close to that of the Gospels.[6]

The solemn opening sentence of Pseudo-Dionysius's book on the Celestial Hierarchy runs as follows, 'Every inspiration from God enters by grace into the world subordinate to Providence, as many-coloured light which yet remains unified. But still more, it transforms the beings into which it radiates into a unity.'

We know that Suger consciously created his church in the image of Dionysius's mystical vision. It was his intention that the stained glass windows should concretize the splendour of the many-coloured light which, streaming through the transparent walls of the Gothic church, would become unified again in its luminous cosmos, imparting unity to all within it.

It is striking that the prologue to the Gospel according to St John and the Gothic worship of light were introduced into the Roman Church in the middle of the twelfth century—just at the time when the conflict with the Cathars was coming to a head. This would suggest that the Church acted again as she had done before when fighting a rival: she took possession of the enemy's most precious treasure—in this instance, light. This would seem to be borne out by the fact that Suger and Bernard of Clairvaux worked closely together, and that Bernard, himself a mystic, spoke of his experience of oneness as a union with the *Logos*.[7]

Denis de Rougemont offers the theory that the troubadours were Cathars.[8] At any rate it is striking that Dante placed among the sodomites the two troubadours he met in purgatory, Guido Guinizelli and Arnaut Daniel, whom he addresses so respectfully and lovingly. Guido first points out to Dante a group of passive sodomites:

> The folk who walk apart from us committed the sin, which erst caused Caesar in his triumph to hear himself reviled with the name of 'Queen'. For this cause, when they depart, they exclaim 'Sodom', upbraiding themselves, as thou hast heard, and promote by their shame the operation of the fire.

Then he says about his own group:

> Our sin was hermaphrodite; but since we observed not the law ordained for man, being led like beasts by our desires, when we depart, to mark our ignominy we recite the name of her who made herself brutish within the wooden cow.[9]

It is worth noting that Dante does not regard sodomy with such severity as to make him place these sinners in hell. They are in purgatory eagerly submitting themselves to the painful purification through which finally they will gain access to paradise.

So among the Gnostics, as in pre-Christian antiquity, homosexual acts were accepted forms of erotic outlet. As such they served primarily to satisfy the senses without necessarily having any symbolic significance. But when sodomy was used as a means of liberation from the constraints of the papal Church, the laws of Jahve, or darkness, then the sodomitic act was genuinely symbolic and to be viewed as having a parallel — though with a different content — in Dorian paiderasty. As with the Dorians the two fundamentally different meanings of the single act could not always be kept clearly apart.

As a result of these developments over this long period from the time of the Christianization of the Roman Empire to the middle of the thirteenth century, homosexual acts were firmly classified as expressions of perversion. Homosexuality went together with heresy and an asocial attitude — not altogether unjustifiably — and was treated accordingly when it appeared openly and assertively. Thus the Hellenistic Gnostics and the medieval Manichees had the effect on the Church of strengthening its prejudice against homosexuality.

Again it should be stressed, however, that the medieval Church apparently did not deliver sodomites to the punishment of the secular arm except when heresy was the main accusation. Homosexual acts in ordinary daily life, numerous as they must have been, were regarded as requiring penance only.

NOTES

1. Plato, *Symposium*, 210–11.
2. Hans Jonas, *The Gnostic Religion* (Boston, 1963), p. 270 ff.

3. Steven Runciman, *The Medieval Manichee* (Cambridge, 1960).
4. Hugh Ross Williamson, *The Arrow and the Sword* (London, 1955), pp. 40–41, and Otto von Simson, *The Gothic Cathedral* (London, 1956), p. 55.
5. Acts XVII, 34.
6. Otto von Simson, *The Gothic Cathedral* (London, 1956), chs. 2, 3, 4.
7. Dom Cuthbert Butler, *Western Mysticism* (London, 1951), pp. 101–102.
8. Denis de Rougemont, *Passion and Society* (London, 1962), chs. 6, 7, 8.
9. Dante, *Purgatory*, translated by Rev. H. F. Tozer (Oxford, 1904), song 26, lines 76 ff.

16

The Witch Cult

Figure 22, a woodcut dating from the beginning of the seventeenth century, depicts a witches' Sabbath and illustrates some important features of the witch cult, the object of severe persecution in France, Germany, the Netherlands, England, Scotland and Scandinavia in the sixteenth and seventeenth centuries. In the picture twelve men and women are grouped around a devil. One of the men plays a flute, the rest dance, holding hands, in a circle around the devil who is phallic, horned and has goat's legs.

It is to the credit of Margaret Murray[1] that she demonstrated the existence in western Europe of a veritable witch cult, composed of heretics hostile to the Church. It used to be believed that the persecutions were due solely to religious superstition, and that the confessions of the witches were extracted under torture, or, if given voluntarily, were the products of the fantasies and dreams of poor hysterical women. Of course these beliefs have some foundation, but there is enough recorded evidence of trials to show convincingly that in the main the Church was faced with actual heresy.

Margaret Murray has made studies of the records of trials in England, Scotland and France. From the French trials she refers in particular to the documents of the Inquisition and especially to those of one of the Inquisitors, Pierre de Lancre. He worked in Labourd in 1609, and he reported his bloody accomplishments scrupulously and in detail. His documents have been among the main sources for investigators in this field.[2]

The records of trials were commonly considered unreliable on the grounds that the confessions were responses to leading questions made under severe torture. However, as Margaret Murray points out,[3] torture was not permitted in England, and, contrary to the practice of other countries, the accused was allowed to plead not guilty. (On the whole England was moderate in its policy. Only about one thousand persons are said to have perished throughout the whole period compared to one hundred thousand in Germany. Also, those found guilty were hanged, not burned alive, and many of the accused were acquitted.[4] In America the trials were few and came late.) Voluntary confessions exist by witches who, like the Christian martyrs, abandoned themselves headlong to their fate, eager to die for their creed and their god. It is notable that the confessions made at English trials agree on important points with those obtained under torture in other countries. Furthermore, Miss Murray states that the inquisitors were bound to be eager to obtain reliable information for use in other trials, a factor not to be overlooked; they also received information from witches who had renounced their beliefs and who confessed voluntarily. The inquisitors must have had a fair knowledge of their 'enemies' in order to be able to formulate their leading questions. So while in many individual cases a person's guilt might be far from established, nevertheless there can be no doubt of the actual existence of a widespread witch cult.

In some places, at least, the witches organized themselves into covens of twelve, centred on a god. The god, as is known from numerous descriptions, was horned and phallic. When in 1484 Innocent VIII issued his Papal bull, setting in motion the persecution of the witches, he confirmed in no uncertain terms that it was fertility magic that the witches were performing. Cults of this kind are always phallic. The Papal bull runs as follows:

It has come to our ears that numbers of both sexes do not avoid to have intercourse with demons, Incubi and Succubi; and that by their sorceries, and by their incantations, charms, and conjurations, they suffocate, extinguish, and cause to perish the births of women, the increase of animals, the corn of the ground, the grapes of the vineyard and the fruit of the trees, as well as men, women, flocks, herds, and other various kinds of animals, vines and apple trees, grass, corn and other fruits of the earth; making and procuring that men and women, flocks and herds and other animals shall suffer and be tormented both from within and without, so that men beget not, nor women conceive; and they impede the conjugal action of men and women.[5]

As was to be expected, the Church ascribed only a destructive purpose to the cult, and the Pope turned its motive upside down. Besides, from an ecclesiastical point of view it made no difference whether a witch used her powers for good or evil. In either case she had them from the Devil, and was therefore guilty whatever the circumstance.

At the same time Innocent sent to Germany his two 'bloodhounds', Kramer and Sprenger — later famous as the authors of *Malleus Maleficarum* (*The Hammer of Witches*) — and they were responsible for starting the avalanche of persecution which was to ravage both Catholic and Protestant countries for centuries.

Parenthetically, it should be pointed out that the current expression, 'the witch hunts of the Middle Ages', is entirely incorrect. The Middle Ages, that is the period before 1450, knew the persecution of heretics — in southern France in particular — but not witch hunts. In Scandinavia there was no persecution of heretics during the Middle Ages, and the first witch was burned in 1539, three years after the Lutheran Reformation.

To return to the phallic witch cult, Margaret Murray demonstrates by means of numerous quotations from the actual trials

L

that the god of the witches was a phallic god, and that the women
had intercourse with him at their Sabbaths. (I have found no
information about the phallic-cultic roles of male witches.) It is
obvious that in most cases this was a ritual copulation and was not
for the satisfaction of the flesh. One after another the witches
described how the god's member was 'so cold, so cold'; they said
that it was bigger than that of a normal man, that the intercourse
was painful, and that his emission was 'icy'. Pregnancy did not
ensue except in a few cases, the woman then having no complaints
of coldness or pain. It is Miss Murray's opinion that, just as the
god appeared clad in the skin of an animal — often that of a goat —
so, too, he was equipped with an artificial phallus as a ritual
remedy. It sounds plausible. Artificial phalli as part of a cultic
equipment are well known from ancient Greece (see Chapter 3).

I have been concerned mainly with tracing the occurrence of
the phallic symbol. It should be stressed in this connection that it
is, after all, of minor importance whether the witches believed in
a phallic god and worshipped him, or whether the Inquisition
and the rest of the population invented him — the populace at
least believed in earnest in the Horned One. Whether the belief
of one or both parties was genuine, the Church's fanaticism
testifies to the power of the phallic symbol. The Horned One
with its grotesque phallic equipment is seen often enough in
fifteenth-century murals in Scandinavian churches, painted long
before witch-hunting started there. It is interesting to note,
incidentally, that for half a century after the beginning of the
German witch hunt until the Reformation in 1536, the Catholic
Church in Denmark preserved its balanced and habitually tolerant
attitude. No persecutions occurred, though the most horrifying
conditions prevailed south of the border in Germany. It fell to the
Reformed Church to let loose the forces of Hell in Denmark after
1536.

Reverting to the scene depicted in Figure 22, we find a clear
reference by a contemporary — Shakespeare — to similar nightly

enterprises in the woods, the dance in Windsor Park in *The Merry Wives of Windsor*. In the play, the ladies Ford and Quickly at first ridicule Falstaff by dressing him as a notorious local witch. Falstaff becomes afraid that the sheriff may seize him as a witch. Then they promise that he can have his way with Mistress Ford if, dressed as the horned hunter—Herne the Hunter—he meets her in Windsor Park between midnight and one o'clock. At the appointed hour, everybody goes to the park to dance around the old oak. It is obvious that Shakespeare is alluding to the actual copulation in the woods between the horned god and women which everybody of his time knew to take place.

Margaret Murray mentions several sources from England's early history which prove the existence of a phallic cult. For instance the priest of Inverkeithing was summoned before the bishop in 1282, because at Easter he had been leading a fertility dance around the phallic figure of a god. As the Church at that time was moderate and unfanatical he was allowed to retain his benefice.[6] And, in the seventh century, the Archbishop of Canterbury issued the following decree, 'If anyone at the kalends of January goes about as a stag or a bull; that is, making himself into a wild animal and dressing in the skin of a herd animal, and putting on the heads of beasts; those who in such wise transform themselves into the appearance of a wild animal: penance for three years because this is devilish.'[7] A transformation of a man into a wild animal such as that described by the Archbishop can be seen in Figure 24, a Scandinavian Bronze Age petroglyph of a phallic man dressed in the skin of an ox with horns and tail.

The phallic symbol appears clearly in the witch cult. On the other hand, the fight against the witch cult was to help harden that suppressive attitude towards openly recognized phallic symbolism which is so characteristic of the civilization of more recent times.

NOTES

1. M. A. Murray, *The Witch Cult in Western Europe* (Oxford, 1962), first published 1921.
2. Julio Caro Baroja, *The World of Witches* (London, 1964). First published in Spanish 1961.
3. M. A. Murray, op. cit.
4. Ronald Seth, *In the Name of the Devil* (London, 1969), p. 11.
5. M. A. Murray, op. cit., p. 24.
6. Op. cit., p. 23.
7. Op. cit., p. 21.

A note on Margaret Murray.

In the works of this gifted and scholarly author, offering so much that is original, it is necessary to draw a clear distinction between the documented material she has brought to light, and the conclusions she draws from it. The first of her books, *The Witch Cult in Western Europe*, the only one to which I refer, offers a wealth of information, solidly documented, with many long, detailed transcripts from the trial records. As to her conclusions I have only used those which I would have drawn myself. The rest—her ideas of a Dianic cult and the survival of ancient religions preserved by the descendants of the 'Pelasgans' of the different countries—I find neither convincing nor necessary. In her later books, such as *The Divine King in England*, the very far-fetched conclusions are so predominant that the interesting and important material which the book contains is nearly swamped by them.

17

Notes on the Phallus and Homosexuality in the Post-medieval West

It is curious that at the same time as the Church and the secular state were waging a common war against the phallic witch cult, a grotesque expression of phallic symbolism emerged in the male dress of the sixteenth century. While the suits of armour lost the slender elegance which the Gothic ones had possessed a new excrescence developed below the breastplate — the cod-piece (Figure 25). It was a conspicuous representation of a penis, big and arching upwards. It cannot have had any practical significance, but was meant as a phallic exhibition, a demonstration of power, a threat signal of the same nature as the helmets hammered into the shape of lion masks which appeared simultaneously. The man in armour with his cod-piece and the baboon exhibiting his erect penis as an aggressive signal to other baboons to keep off aim at the same effect. This phallic attribute was also used on ordinary clothing; the frontispiece to this book shows an example typical of that time. Notice the solemn bearing and dignified expression of the duke, precluding any idea of obscenity in connection with his mighty red cod-piece. The latter is a condensed expression of those eminent qualities as a man and a prince which he wished to convey to the world.

As far as I know the cod-piece of the sixteenth century is the last expression in our civilization of phallic symbolism openly displayed and publicly recognized and accepted. Shakespeare already seems to be viewing the cod-piece as something comical, since the fool is the only person in *King Lear* expressly said to wear one.

In sixteenth-century drawings the *Commedia dell' arte* figure of Pantalone often appears conspicuously phallic,[1] and in southern Europe phallic amulets are still in use, just as the *fica*—a gesture made by extending the fist with the thumb protruding between the second and third fingers—is a phallic representation used as a magic defence against the evil eye and other dangers.[2]

However, in New Guinea the otherwise completely naked Papuan warrior of today wears a 'cod-piece' when armed for warfare. These cod-pieces are made of straw, conspicuously painted in red or yellow, and are certainly not meant to conceal the penis. On the contrary, they are just as aggressively exhibitionistic as the European cod-pieces of the sixteenth century. They exist in a variety of forms, Figure 28 showing one typical example.

As to homosexual acts, I have already mentioned that the attitude of the secular authorities during the Middle Ages seems to have been not to prosecute the offenders. Sexual transgressions were ecclesiastical sins, and capital punishment could not be inflicted unless the Church handed over the sinner to the secular arm; and—so it appears—the medieval Church did not do this unless the primary crime was heresy.

However, in the sixteenth and seventeenth centuries secular legislation made its appearance; and the ensuing judicial practice must to some extent reflect the general attitude to homosexual acts held by our societies since that time. It is therefore worth examining some of the more outstanding features of the historical development within this field in various European countries up to the present day.

In the case of England this development has been clearly charted in a recent book by H. Montgomery Hyde.[3] He takes as his point of departure Henry VIII's Act of 1533 in which 'the detestable and abominable Vice of Buggery' was made a felony, punishable with death by hanging. The wording of the Preamble to the Act is most important historically in that it shows how sodomy had previously been treated in England as in other countries during the Middle Ages as an ecclesiastical sin only, '... the temporal courts had not punished it and ... no one had been put to death for it for a very long time past.'[4]

It must not be thought, however, that this change in the law necessarily betokened a hardening of the general moral attitude. As Montgomery Hyde points out:

The Statute (25 Henry VIII, c. 6) was not occasioned by any particular desire on the part of the king and his chief minister, Thomas Cromwell, who piloted it through Parliament, to clamp down on homosexuals. Its primary object was part of Henry's policy in general towards the Church. Besides the seizure of its property, this included the progressive reduction of the jurisdiction of the ecclesiastical courts, by withdrawing from them the right to try certain offences which were now regarded as temporal and were henceforth to become felonies triable in the ordinary courts. No doubt buggery appeared to Cromwell as suitable a subject as any other for the inauguration of this process which was to continue and eventually lead to the practical abolition of all ecclesiastical courts a century later.[5]

It was to be a long time still before the law actively prosecuted homosexuality as such. This is borne out by the fact that no court case on a charge of buggery between adult males is known in the next century, although during that period a great number of persons suffered death for other kinds of felony. The first recorded trial on account of buggery is that of Lord Castlehaven before the House of Lords in 1631. Castlehaven's was a quite extra-ordinary case. He was charged by his own son with both sodomy in relation to several of his servants and rape of his wife and of his daughter-in-law. Allegedly he ordered his servants to commit the rapes while he looked on, occasionally lending a hand to hold down the ladies. He was convicted and sentenced to be hanged, but because he was a peer descended from a long line of men who had performed valuable services for the Crown, the hanging was commuted to beheading. He met his end on Tower Hill 'with dignity and courage'. Two of his servants who had witnessed against him — thereby accusing themselves — were convicted too and hanged at Tyburn. In his speech before the gallows one of them repeated his confession: his lordship had buggered him, and he his lordship.

Nine years later another peer, the Lord Bishop of Waterford and Lismore in Ireland, was convicted of buggery with his tithe proctor. Both were hanged. From this date numerous prosecutions for homosexuality between consenting adults are recorded throughout the seventeenth, eighteenth, nineteenth and twentieth centuries up until 1967. (Incidentally, the motives for bringing these charges seem to have been entirely moral, and in no degree political.) All strata of society were involved, not least schools and universities. Death sentences and executions were frequent. If the accused were wealthy enough to be released on bail and then absconded and avoided trial, they had to spend the rest of their lives abroad. Reprieves were rare; over considerable periods of time four out of five convicted were executed, as compared, for example, to one out of eight other capital offenders in 1811.[6] In 1806 five of the most respectable and affluent middle-aged citizens of Warrington were sentenced; two of them were granted respite, but the remaining three were hanged 'in a state of the greatest agitation'.[7]

It was the general rule that the courts required proof of pene-tration. Cases of emission of seed on the body but with no penctration proved were regarded as 'attempts' and punished by an hour in the pillory plus payment of a fine and imprisonment. To be pilloried was a serious punishment for, apart from the humiliation, there was a real risk of being badly injured or even killed by the brickbats hurled by the mob.

After 1836 no death sentence was carried out, and in 1861 capital punishment was replaced by penal servitude for life or for any term of not less than ten years at the discretion of the courts. The requirement of proof of penetration was re-enacted. This law remained in force until 1967.

It is to be noted that homosexual acts other than anal inter-course—manual or oral practices (fellatio), for instance—were not punishable by the law. However, in 1885 a most important amendment was introduced, which was to have far-reaching consequences. In the late hours of the evening at a thinly attended House of Commons session it was agreed to include in the law a clause by which 'an act of gross indecency' with another man, or attempts to procure the commission by another male of any such act, not amounting to buggery, whether in public or private, was made an offence punishable by up to two years' imprison-ment with hard labour. The vague term 'gross indecency' was particularly unfortunate as were the words 'in private' and the phrase with regard to procuration, the latter paving the way for the charge of 'importuning' which was to be used so freely by the police. From then on, until 1967, any inverse homosexual was in the gravest danger of prosecution, imprisonment, social ruin and blackmail. The witch hunt became unrestricted.

During the late nineteen forties and the early 'fifties the number of cases of sodomy, attempts to commit 'unnatural offences', 'importuning', and offences of 'gross indecency between males' rose steeply, reaching a peak in 1953-4. Montgomery Hyde argues convincingly that this increase was due to an excess of zeal on the part of the police, bringing an intensification of interest, for instance, in what took place in the many public urinals and lavatories. Young, attractive policemen in plain clothes were even used as *agents provocateurs*.

The intolerable conditions resulting and the ensuing heavy public criticism eventually led to the setting up of the Wolfenden Committee in 1954. In 1957 the Committee, headed by Sir John Wolfenden, submitted its report. Its recommendations cut the ground from under the feet of the law; it advocated that homosexual acts between consenting males above the age of twenty-one, committed in private, should no longer be considered a punishable offence. Since the report expressly stated that no convincing evidence had been found in support of the contention that seduction in youth was a decisive factor in the later development of homosexuality as a condition, the high age-level of twenty-one was probably recommended to make the change in the law more easily acceptable to the general public—and to the Government and members of the House of Commons.

In these last respects the report and its many supporters were not to attain their goal for another ten years. Both Mr Butler as Home Secretary and later Sir Alec Douglas-Home as Prime Minister maintained that the balance of Parliamentary and public opinion was not in favour of amending the law. It was left to the House of Lords finally to take up the matter and initiate the changes proposed in the Wolfenden Report.* Now the House of Commons followed the House of Lords and in 1967 royal assent was given to the bill, by which homosexual acts between consenting adults over the age of twenty-one, committed in private, were no longer punishable. However, the Navy and the Merchant Marine were exempt, and in Scotland and Northern Ireland the old law is still in force.

It is interesting that the Labour Prime Minister Mr Wilson

---

* Some expressions of diehard resistance were voiced in the House of Lords, led by Viscount Montgomery of Alamein. 'To condone unnatural offences in male persons over twenty-one or, indeed, in male persons of any age, seems to me utterly wrong . . . a weakening of the law will strike a blow at all those devoted people who are working to improve the moral fibre of the youth of this country. And heaven knows, it wants improving!'[8] the noble Lord protested.

preferred not to vote at the final division in the House of Commons. It was the House of Lords which took a firm stand on the matter. Butler, Douglas-Home, and Wilson seemed to exhibit — as for a long time did the majority of M.P.s — an immoderate concern for public opinion in the teeth of convincing professional evidence; they showed the politicians' fear of doing anything that might harm their chances of success at the next election. In some circumstances it would seem to be an advantage to have, alongside the elected legislative body, another assembly whose members retain their seats, once obtained, without having to consider their popularity with the voters. In the same context it should be remembered that in 1921 when a proposal to make homosexual legislation applicable to women had been passed in the House of Commons by a large majority (Winston Churchill and Stanley Baldwin voted against it), it was the House of Lords that prevented it.

Mr Montgomery Hyde's book ought to be read widely, not least because of the illustration it affords of the fact that the time since the Renaissance has not been in every respect a period of progress, enlightenment and humanization.

The innumerable executions and heavy prison sentences for homosexuality in England from 1631 onwards reflect a harsh attitude towards homosexual acts over the last three hundred and fifty years. (It is worth comparing with the corresponding period in Danish–Norwegian history which is dealt with below.) Nevertheless it is something of an open secret that in former as well as recent times homosexual acts occurred, and probably still occur, with considerable frequency, in English public schools, the most renowned of which are certainly not exempt. The memoirs of known and respected men speak of this freely. Even the fact that the boys often take the initiative towards their elders has been attested.[9]

The largest proportion of homosexual relationships in public schools between boys, boys and youths, or boys and their masters is bound to involve boys who have an average heterosexual career later. It is a fact that male prowess is much cultivated as part of the traditional system of education in British public schools. Those who excel in the desirable masculine qualities are the objects of admiration and hero worship. It has to be recognized, I think, that, as in Greece, a style of life and upbringing of this kind is necessarily linked with homosexual feelings, whether or not expressed in action. Paradoxical as it may sound, such 'normal' homosexuality is likely to have contributed to the creation of the type of man who was essential to the formation of the British Empire.

In France people were burned for homosexual acts up to the end of the eighteenth century (a relic, possibly, of the fight against the Cathars), but soon afterwards the *Code Pénal Napoléon* (1810) abolished the laws against sexual relations between consenting adults of the same sex.

In Germany the laws introduced in the sixteenth century in the different independent states decreed death by burning as the punishment for sodomy. Simson and Geerds[10] who give this and the following information do not tell us how extensive were the prosecutions carried out according to these laws. However, during the thirty-year period from 1811 a number of the German states followed the example of Napoleon's Code of 1810 and abolished the legislation against homosexuality between consenting adults. Prussia was an exception, and when in 1871 Germany was united under her leadership the Prussian law was made valid for the realm as a whole. However, only coitus-like acts were punishable. It was not till 1935 under the National-Socialist rule that an amendment similar to the English one of 1885 was brought in. Hitler used it freely and very much for political purposes. Over the three-year period 1931–3, 2,319 men were convicted. During the three-year period 1937–9, after the amendment, the number multiplied by ten, to 24,447. In addition an untold number of persons in or outside the Nazi Party were whisked away to the concentration camps without trial, on suspicion alone. This law is still in force, although it is likely to be repealed in the not too distant future.

The attitude in Denmark during the Middle Ages has already been discussed. On February 2nd, 1227, the Pope wrote a letter to the Danish archbishop in reply to his request for advice on how to deal with a number of persons, both clerical and secular, within his see who had had unlawful intercourse 'not only with their next of kin, but even with beasts and other men' (note that intercourse between women is not mentioned). Partly because of bashfulness, and partly on account of the length and hazardous nature of the journey, the archbishop felt that they could not very well go to Rome. The Pope gave the archbishop the authority to decide for himself on a penance which should be neither too hard nor too lenient.[11] Obviously the issue here is one of ecclesiastical penance only, and the consideration shown by the archbishop towards the sinners is noticeable – he feels sorry that they should have to undertake the long, dangerous journey to Rome and appear before the Pope on such an account. And the Pope advises him to use moderation when prescribing the penance. The secular authorities are not even mentioned.

The official attitude of the judiciary in the Denmark of the seventeenth and eighteenth centuries is set down in the Danish Lawbook of King Christian V of 1683. In accordance with Leviticus it lays down that, 'Intercourse against nature shall be punished by burning.'[12] The law applies to both intercourse with animals and sodomy.

However, it is striking that while prosecution for bestiality – crimen bestialitatis – was by no means rare, only a single example of prosecution for homosexuality is known. Georg Hansen, who studied the moral attitudes in Denmark of the seventeenth and eighteenth centuries,[13] found numerous court cases of bestiality, but not a single case of homosexuality.

Knud Waaben informs me that he knows of only one court case of pederasty from this period. In 1744 a weaver was sentenced to two years forced labour followed by banishment from the province of Jutland, because he had had unnatural intercourse with a boy. The latter was released after a period of detention during the trial. The weaver was married.[14] His sentence was at variance with the provisions of the Danish Lawbook. In the early days not many sentences were recorded in print, and therefore it may well be that other cases exist which will be discovered at some later date.

This applies in Norway, also, both before and after the separation from Denmark in 1814. A Norwegian textbook of penal law, issued in 1849, contains the following statement: 'The author knows of only one case of prosecution for pederasty'— and the accused was acquitted.[15] After 1815 the death sentence on all who were found guilty of 'intercourse against nature' was commuted to forced labour— the Norwegian Lawbook of Christian V, king of Denmark and Norway, was a replica of the Danish Lawbook— and in the Protocol of Pardons of the Norwegian Judicial Department ten cases of bestiality are found during the period 1814–31, but no case of homosexuality.[16]

It seems most likely that nobody was interested in bringing charges against persons committing homosexual acts. Not that the official attitude was in any way in doubt. It was plainly expressed by Ludvig Holberg.* In 1716, on his return to Denmark from two years' study in Oxford he published his *Introduction to Natural and International Law*. This was a textbook very much in the style of *De officiis hominis et civis* (a guide to man's duties both as an individual and as a citizen) published in 1673 by the German writer on jurisprudence, Samuel Pufendorf.[17]

Holberg acknowledges his debt to Pufendorf who, in turn, was

---

* Holberg was a professor at the University of Copenhagen, a historian, moral philosopher and, in later life, a comic poet and playwright whose plays are still regularly performed.

influenced by the enlightened approach of the Dutch lawyer Hugo Grotius[18] and also by Thomas Hobbes's less optimistic view of man. In other words, Holberg's *Introduction* reflects the views of these eminent philosophers rather than local conditions. By and large the points of view he puts forward may be regarded as representative of those widely held in the leading circles of Europe.

His principles with regard to homosexuality are unmistakeable. Because God has implanted in man a natural inclination towards the opposite sex, 'we must condemn the wicked vice in those who seek intercourse with beasts or with persons of their own sex which, in the old days, was so common amongst the Greeks that not even public laws could put an end to the habit.'[19]

However, at a time when for centuries servants had been sleeping together in the same bed, man with man and man with boy (the custom being on the whole that persons of the same sex shared beds, adults as well as children), it cannot possibly have been considered politic to investigate what was happening in the various beds — particularly since zeal displayed in this direction would bring about criminal prosecutions of staggering dimensions. This evaluation finds support in the following words of Holberg:

Finally, the authorities cannot punish vices which are practised by so many, and which are so firmly embedded that to uproot the evil would be to cause the disintegration of the whole state. And if they are but deeds of darkness and are not generally noticed and therefore of little consequence, why trouble the authorities by calling their attention to them?[20]

Besides, in Holberg's time there was little of the anxiety commonly felt today about the harm to children's development resulting from sexual molestation by grown men.

So the apparent absence of criminal cases dealing with homosexual offences in seventeenth- and eighteenth-century Denmark

–Norway (though the punishment for bestiality was carried out in all its harshness) seems to indicate that society in general shied away from applying to everyday occurrences the hard Mosaic principles of the penal codes.

However, the penal code of 1866, abolishing capital punishment for homosexual offences and substituting imprisonment, brought about a noticeable change. From now on a considerable number of sentences were passed on homosexuals in Denmark. So the tempering of the punishment for unnatural intercourse, humane though it looks, did in fact lead to a sharpening of the judicial practice with many more frequent prosecutions, since the punishment did not seem so completely inhuman any more. It was probably the inverse homosexuals who were predominantly the victims.

Again it is interesting that the provisions of the Danish Penal Code of 1866 with regard to homosexuality only applied to men. C. Goos, the leading Danish authority of the late nineteenth century, expressly stated that nothing in the law warrants the institution of legal proceedings against women for homosexual acts.[21] This is representative of practically all penal codes from the Laws of Moses onwards, the Austrian Code being an isolated exception. Regardless of the general status of equality of women nowadays, the role of sexual offender is still reserved for men.

In Denmark the number of prosecutions decreased considerably during the first three decades of the twentieth century, and in 1932 the law was abolished. A grown person is now only punishable on account of homosexuality if his partner is a minor, that is under the age of eighteen.

In these brief accounts one is struck by several outstanding features. For instance, in England and Denmark, it is clear that in the Middle Ages the secular authorities took no notice of sexual acts between males; they remained ecclesiastical sins, and nobody suffered the death penalty or received any other secular punishment for them.

However, in the post-Renaissance period a change took place. Legislation was introduced, in England in 1533, in Denmark in 1683, making 'buggery' in England and 'unnatural intercourse' in Denmark punishable by death — by hanging and burning respectively. Now it is obvious that until the latter part of the nineteenth century only acts of anal penetration were the target of these laws. In the case of England this is well attested not only by the use of the word 'buggery' as the legal term, but also by its being expressly stated in numerous cases that the courts insisted on proof of anal penetration. For instance, in 1817 a man was convicted and sentenced to death for having with his fingers forced open the mouth of a seven-year-old boy, put his penis into it, and had an emission. However, the judge postponed the execution until the opinion of his fellow judges could be heard as to whether or not the act constituted buggery. They held that it did not, and the prisoner received a free pardon.[22] (Consider the change in attitude which has taken place in the short span from then till now.) From the wording of the Danish Lawbook and the inclusion of bestiality in the same clause it is likely that what was meant by 'unnatural intercourse' was anal penetration in Denmark as in England. (Of course we lack the testimony of trial records in Denmark.) At any rate it is clear that there existed a variety of sexual acts leading to orgasm, committed between males, which were legally ignored before the last decades of the nineteenth century.

Sodomy is the homosexual act which carries a dominance-submission symbolism. Could it be that in some way the powerful emotions and ideas connected with this symbolism were responsible for the fact that, among the various forms of homosexual relations, only sodomy became the object of public attention and was criminalized during the period from the seventeenth century to the latter part of the nineteenth? It is tempting to speculate — though at present one can do no more. It might also be that the excess of religious zeal after the Reformation brought with it an

M

enforced obedience to the law of Holy Scripture which specifically prohibits sodomy. The general surge of antisexual moralism in the latter half of the nineteenth century could be the factor responsible for the changes in attitude to homosexual acts in general which took place at that time.

Again it is striking that though Danish and English legislation in the late seventeenth and the eighteenth century followed identical principles, only a single case—and that so leniently treated as to be at odds with the law—has been unearthed in Denmark; while in England the many cases of sodomy which are known from the same period were punished with the full severity of the law. Both were Protestant countries, and the general moral attitude of the time in Denmark was unlikely to have been laxer than in England. Neither is it conceivable that Danes were less prone to commit sodomitic acts than Englishmen. I can offer no explanation of this difference in the judicial practices of England and Denmark.

Be that as it may, it seems that until a change occurred in the nineteenth century sexual acts between males, other than sodomy, were not seriously condemned. Most likely they were overlooked, condoned or regarded with indifference. One is tempted to draw the conclusion that under such circumstances homosexual impulses cannot have been repressed in the way that they are now.

So apparently our present wholesale banishment of homosexual phenomena from the life of the 'normal' male is comparatively recent. It began somewhere in the nineteenth century and manifested itself judicially in England after the passing of the amendment of 1885 and in Denmark probably during the years after the law of 1866. Suppression and repression of homosexual tendencies in normal men accompanied this development—whether as a cause or as a consequence of it is hard to say. After having caused their due measures of suffering these laws were reformed: radically in Denmark in 1932, partially in England thirty-five years later. (The English age of consent of twenty-one is a very high one, and the law still provides grounds for the charge of 'importuning'.) However, these reforms are predominantly and deservedly for the benefit of the inverse homosexuals. The repressions and denials which our present civilization seems to develop in 'normal' men are not likely to be affected by them. Some considerations regarding this last point follow in the final chapter.

Although extrinsic to the main topic of this book, I would like to comment briefly on the severity and zeal with which bestiality was punished in Denmark. To be burnt alive on a pyre was the punishment for anyone found guilty of this crime. A decree of 1711 laid down that the convicted were to be strangled before burning. The animal was to be killed too. It may contribute to the understanding of this cruel and merciless punishment to know that bestiality has a part in many religious cults, even today, as it had in Denmark in pre-Christian times, and certainly during the Bronze Age. Evidence of this may be seen in Figure 26, a petroglyph reproducing a cultic scene of a man's copulation with a cow. A similar scene of a man and a donkey was found on a North Italian Bronze Age rock-carving. It was usual for the Christian Church to treat with particular severity any elements of a previous cult which it did not choose to adopt. An attitude of condemnation, even disgust, was inculcated in people by the Church, often to last for centuries, long after the pre-Christian cultic element had been forgotten. There is a curious example of this in Denmark. The horse was foremost among the sacrificial animals in pre-Christian times, and the meat of the sacrificial animal was eaten at religious festivals. We know that during the interim period finally leading to the acceptance of Christianity in the North, the eating of horse-meat was a particular issue, the Church being eager to see this very important heathen custom abolished. After some difficulty the Church was successful, and to this day most people refuse to eat this very tasty meat.

NOTES

1. Allardyce Nicoll, *The World of Harlequin* (Cambridge, 1963), figs. 27, 29, 30.
2. S. Seligmann, *Der böse Blich und Verwandtes* (Berlin, 1910). (Vol. II shows many *ficas* and phallic amulets in figs. 176–90.)
3. H. Montgomery Hyde, *The Other Love* (London, 1970).
4. Op. cit., p. 38.
5. Op. cit., p. 39.
6. Op. cit., p. 78.
7. Op. cit., p. 78.
8. Op. cit., p. 262.
9. Op. cit., p. 199.
10. Simson-Geerds, *Straftaten gegen die Person und Sittlichkeitsdelikte in rechtsvergleichender Sicht* (Munich, 1969), p. 422 ff.
11. The Papal letter in Latin can be found in A. Krarup, *Bullarium Danicum* (Copenhagen, 1932), p. 178.
12. The Danish Law Book, 6, 13, 15.
13. Georg Hansen, *Sædelighedsforhold blandt Landbefolkningen i Danmark i det 18. aarhundrede* (Copenhagen, 1957).
14. J. R. Hübertz, *Aktstykker vedkommende Staden og Stiftet, Aarhus*, Vol. III, 1846, p. 325.
15. P. C. Lassen, *Haandbog i Criminalretten* (Christiania, 1849), part I, p. 226, note.
16. H. A. Th. Dedichen, 'Om homoseksualitet' (*Tidsskrift for nordisk retsmedicin og psykiatri*), VI, (1906), pp. 154–5.
17. Samuel Pufendorf, *De Jure Naturae et Gentium* (1672).
18. Hugo Grotius, *De Jure Belli et Pacis* (1625).
19. Ludvig Holberg, *Naturens og Folke-Rettens Kundskab*, quoted from F. J. Billeskov Jansen's edition of Holberg (Copenhagen, 1969), I, p. 250.
20. Op. cit., p. 323.
21. C. Goos, *Den danske Strafferet* (Copenhagen, 1895), part I, pp. 547–8.
22. H. Montgomery Hyde, op. cit., p. 8.

CONCLUSION

18

The Breakdown of Gustav von Aschenbach

From previous chapters the fact will have emerged that a homosexual radical exists ubiquitously in men, a radical which may manifest itself openly and unmasked, or which may operate only beyond the boundaries of consciousness. A comparison between the Dorian Greeks and the men of our own European-American civilization illustrates the difference between the overt and the hidden existence of this radical. I have dealt with some of the main points of the historical development which caused the homosexual radical to go underground, taking along with it conscious understanding of the phallic symbol. It is reasonable to say that both radical and symbol went underground—their existence there was demonstrated first by Freud—because it has been shown through clinical experience that from their present position outside the boundaries of consciousness they still exert a decisive influence on the life of men.

I have chosen a number of extreme examples to demonstrate that it is possible to distinguish between the erotic and the aggressive aspects of the homosexual radical—in other words that the genital organ of the male may serve both erotic and aggressive aims. Considerable emphasis has been laid on the aggressive aspect, not because it is more important or predominant than the erotic one, but because its nature and function are less generally known.

The erotic aspect played a fundamental cultic role in the Dorian state. Among the Ionian Athenians the part it played was largely personal, aesthetic and ethical. In Rome its significance was purely erotic. In Christian Europe sensual, manifest homosexuality lost acceptance. Nevertheless it would seem likely that homosexual acts, whether more or less hidden, have occurred, to a not inconsiderable extent, among normal men and boys. These acts, having gone unpunished, were therefore undocumented until the advent of modern investigations like that of the Kinsey Report.

To avoid confusion I have only dealt with relations in which an indisputable genital activity exists. Relationships may be genuinely homosexual, however, without any genital involvement. We are used to the idea of non-genital erotic relations between the two sexes, but usually we do not see relationships between persons of the same sex in this light. However, between men and boys, older and younger boys, men of different ages or status as well as between men who are peers, emotional relationships exist having a colour and an intensity which on closer viewing prove to be sexual, although the genital aspect is beyond the relationship and is excluded from the consciousness of the partners.

Numerous such examples are found in feudal Europe between vassal and liege. It is a relationship which has been vividly described in the *Song of Roland*, the legends of King Arthur and his knights and in the poems of the Troubadours—those about Tristan and King Mark, for instance. And the nature of this relationship emerges not only from our study of literature, but from historical sources as well. Such relations were characterized by C. S. Lewis, in his famous book on medieval poetry, in the following terms:

The deepest of worldly emotions in this period is the love of man for man, the mutual love of warriors who die together fighting against odds, and the affection between vassal and lord. We shall never understand this last, if we think of it in the light of our own moderated and impersonal loyalties. We must not think of officers drinking the king's health: we must think rather of a small boy's feeling for some hero in the sixth form ... these male affections — though wholly free from the taint that hangs about 'friendship' in the ancient world — were themselves loverlike; in their intensity, their wilful exclusion of other values, and their uncertainty, they provided an exercise of the spirit not wholly unlike that which later ages have found in 'love'.[1]

The Romantic period abounds in examples of such relationships. From the end of the eighteenth and the beginning of the nineteenth centuries — the sentimental period — innumerable intensely emotional love relations are described poetically or reported historically.

In these relationships open expression was given to heated feelings, and kisses and embraces were frequently exchanged. Friendships and teacher–pupil relationships had a significance and were regarded with a respect difficult for most of us to understand fully.

Great changes took place in the course of the last century, and today friendships between men are generally tempered and more remote. They are regarded as of secondary importance compared to the marital relationship. This was not necessarily the case in former times, when there was no thought of pitting the importance of wife against that of friend, since each relationship was considered valuable in its own right. Nowadays emotional expressions are rare and restrained among men; kissing and embracing is not the rule any longer, as it is still in the East. There is a conspicuous shyness about bodily contact. We have come far from the time when two grown men could sleep naked in the same bed as a matter of course, in a bodily contact as close as that described in Iago's words in the following speech:

... I lay with Cassio lately,
And being troubled with a raging tooth,
I could not sleep.
There are a kind of men so loose of soul,
That in their sleeps will mutter their affairs,
One of this kind is Cassio:
In sleep I heard him say 'Sweet Desdemona,
Let us be wary, let us hide our loves;'
And then, sir, would he gripe and wring my hand,
Cry out, 'O sweet creature!' and then kiss me hard,
As if he pluck'd up kisses by the roots,
That grew upon my lips, then laid his leg
Over my thigh, and sigh'd, and kiss'd, and then
Cried 'Cursed fate, that gave thee to the Moor!'[2]

While we in our Western society are becoming more and more tolerant towards the small percentage of inverse homosexuals, our intolerance of the homosexuality of heterosexual men seems to be ever increasing, not only in its genital but in its non-genital forms. In *Hávamál* (one of the Norse poems of the Edda), it is said that 'men are men's joy'.[3] The full implication of this expression is alien to us; the same is true of the common Norse expression, 'Bare is a brotherless back', depicting the miserable situation of a man standing alone without the faithful backing of good friends. The world of the Norsemen was held together by the close personal bonds with other men through kinship, friendship and the dependence of chieftain and yeoman. There is a chasm between this and modern group solidarity. To the latter, close personal relations present something of a threat; ideally personal bonds are expected to retreat before the considerations of the group and its 'cause' or common interests.

At the beginning of this century Thomas Mann related in a short story how Gustav von Aschenbach met with Death in

Venice. In the figure of Aschenbach he drew the picture of a great European man of letters: a spiritual, thoughtful, profound personality; a man who—after a short-lived marriage, rudely terminated by the death of his wife—was living a lonely, hard-working, frugal life of the strictest self-discipline; a man honoured and respected by his contemporaries for his literary work and ennobled by a German prince in acknowledgement of his accomplishments. Throughout his life he had given the world the impression of being what he wanted to be: the epitome of an Apollonian personality, clear, composed and masterful. On one occasion, however, a man who was a shrewd judge of human nature made a revealing remark about him: ' "You see, Aschenbach has always lived thus," he said, and he closed his hand into a tight fist, "never thus", letting his hand hang comfortably relaxed from the arm of his chair.' There were in fact discrete signs of the presence of some strain within Aschenbach's personality. Usually he kept his head inclined a little to one side in a posture in some way suggestive of suffering. Also a state of inward conflict was reflected by the fact that his main work was a prose epic on the victorious heroship of Frederick the Great, while at the same time he felt deeply attracted by the figure of St Sebastian, the saint who, chained to a pillar and pierced by swords and spears, stood suffering, but proud and unshaken.

One day, exhausted by a concentrated, strenuous, but not very successful morning's work, the ageing author—he was already well past fifty—went out for a walk. When, somewhat tired, he was about to return home, his eye was suddenly caught by an unusual type of man, who seemed from his dress and general appearance to be a traveller; there was an exotic air about him, something strangely informal and self-assured, energetic and powerful; he was bold and courageous-looking, making, even, a somewhat savage impression. Captivated against his will Aschenbach lingered, looking at the man who then returned his gaze, staring straight in to his eyes in a directly militant way as if determined 'to bring matters to a head' and make Aschenbach avert his eyes. Embarrassed, Aschenbach turned and walked away. From then on, however, he felt possessed by a wanderlust, and soon after this incident he departed from Munich to end in Venice. Here on the Lido under a grey sky, in the damp and heavy air, he fell in love, unresistingly, with a delicate, graceful pre-puberal boy — while rumours of a cholera outbreak spread, leaving him unheeding.

He never exchanged a single word with the boy, but tried to keep him in sight as much as possible. He went so far as to follow stealthily behind the boy and his family on their walks through the streets of Venice. He was enchanted, possessed — and his personality began to fall apart.

Finally he had a dream which bereft him of the last remnants of resistance against the Dionysian forces that had broken loose within him — a dream which left his whole existence, his life's culture, shattered.

It began with anxiety — anxiety, lust and an aghast curiosity about what was to come. And it came, advancing through mountainous country, the great Dionysian train with booming din and enticing flute tones, a turmoil of bodies, women waving torches or live snakes, or shrieking and lifting their breasts in both hands, and horned furry men, goats and smooth boys. The mighty phallus was raised, and all raged about it yelling and foaming at the mouth, with rank gestures and lecherous hands, laughing, groaning. They wounded each other, blood flowed, animals were torn asunder, and on the trampled moss they copulated in boundless promiscuity.

Great was his disgust, great his fear; his honest will was to ward off this degradation, so alien and so hostile to his composed and dignified mind. But he succumbed, drugged by lust, raging and blinded, and finally he himself was of it; he became one with the licentious unbridled turmoil, and he tasted lewdness and the rage of destruction.

Von Aschenbach woke up from this dream shaken asunder, powerless, lost to the demon. He had his hair dyed, his eyebrows plucked and his face made up. He no longer considered whether his passion for the boy would attract attention. A few days later he collapsed, dead, in his deck-chair, gazing at the boy on the beach.[4]

Death in Venice is not to be viewed as a record of an odd perversion, a chart of a mental patient. Regardless of the many naturalistic details the story is not naturalistic, and neither is the dream. Mann is relating a myth of universal validity.* From out of his deep insight (he was writing at the same time as Freud, but was still uninfluenced by Freud's ideas) he lucidly exposes a fundamental conflict of the mind in the Europe of recent times.

The passion of a Gustav von Aschenbach cannot have been unknown to Goethe who in his famous poem has 'Erlkönig' ('The King of the Elves') call out to the boy:

> I love you, your beautiful figure arouses me,
> and if you are not willing, then I shall use force.

In Chapter 2 I have described the readiness for homosexual arousal of the average boy and youth, and I pointed out its significance in connection with processes of identification, so indispensable for normal development. I mentioned how easily boys and youths are led into, or bring themselves into, erotic relationships to older persons whom they admire as ideals. I stressed, too, that in the event that some such relationship was found to exist, there would be no reason to assume that this would have disturbing effect on the heterosexual development of the boy. However, as we have seen, it is rare for grown men, apart from the small circle of inverse homosexuals, to indulge in genital

* The novel in general and the dream in particular are obviously reminiscent of Euripides' *Bacchae*, and the dyed and made-up Gustav von Aschenbach calls to mind the debased Pentheus.

relations with each other or with boys under the normal circumstances of our daily life. So the homosexual inclinations of grown men seem to have weakened with maturity, or—to put it perhaps more accurately—grown men show much stronger powers of resistance to them. The change takes place during the age period of twenty to twenty-three, at a time when, in cultures where pederasty is accepted, youths lose their attraction for normal grown men. Incidentally, it is at the same age that youths in our society who prostitute themselves homosexually pass the age limit for this profession.

Grown men in our society seem to have conquered their homosexual tendencies—primarily by channelling their sexual urges exclusively towards women. However strange it may sound we have to acknowledge, nevertheless, that all men have the same disposition as Gustav von Aschenbach and the Dorians. This disposition becomes suppressed and finally repressed on reaching adult life. In most men the repression is so successful that no conscious feeling of want is left. It is mainly in cases of mental unbalance, where other disturbing symptoms are present, that otherwise heterosexual men become conscious of disturbing feelings of homosexual temptation. Breakdowns as serious as that of Gustav von Aschenbach are seen only in cases of severe disturbance, like a schizophrenic development, for instance. But most men in our part of the world go through their adult lives in ignorance of their own homosexuality. It should be mentioned, however, that there are men who have a certain recognition of a well-managed and undisturbing homosexual potential within them. It may be a sign of a particular psychic strength in their personalities.

Tendencies towards genital activity of an aggressive nature are repressed in our present civilization as much as or even more than the erotic ones. Generally speaking the men of our society are not conscious of potentials like those openly expressed in the Near East and—at least verbally—among the ancient Norsemen. This means that conscious understanding of the aggressive aspects of phallic symbolism is lost too; and this in turn means that direct appreciation of the signal function of a phallic symbolism in dominance-submission patterns has disappeared from consciousness—notwithstanding that these patterns still exist unchanged and ready for action below the threshold.

We have lost familiarity not only with phallic symbolism, but also with many of its representations.* Their disappearance from our daily life is closely connected with the revolutionary changes in the social systems of our time. In former times people everywhere in the world were dominated by a distinct hierarchical order—like so many other animals living in troops, flocks and so forth. A society's security and peace, its external strength, and its ability to survive were based on its hierarchical structure. For the longest periods in man's history individuals were born to their station in society and remained there, although considerable flexibility and movement upwards and downwards were found in many places—in England and Scandinavia, for instance.

Directly related to man's hierarchical disposition are signals of dominance and submission. For instance, mounting and presentation are built into him as into the primates, such as baboons. These signals are used in all hierarchical societies to define and maintain the order of the hierarchy. Representations of the original symbols are usually used in human societies; the bared head, the bowed back, the kneeling position, the kiss on the hand are all signals of submission, while the erect posture, the hand raised or extended for the other to bend over, the accolade (still used by the British monarch) are the signs of dominance. It has been shown in an earlier chapter that the original peno-anal attitudes and actions signifying dominance and submission are still found in the dreams of Western man or expressed in action by men in the Near East.

* It may be helpful here to distinguish between a symbol and its representations—for instance, phallus is a symbol, and a spear may be a representation of this symbol.

In recent times we have witnessed how democratic ideals have undermined the old hierarchical structure to such an extent that already its pattern has nearly vanished. The hierarchical nature of men is revealed most markedly today by the loud protests against what remains of its manifestations. Speaking of the British royalty in *Anatomy of Britain Today*, Anthony Sampson by way of comparison points to the democratic King of Denmark who 'bows to his guests'.[5] This could be said to demonstrate prototypically how far Denmark has gone towards abolishing its hierarchy. It also shows in a way representative of Danish society as a whole how the signals of dominance have fallen into disuse. When signals are employed they are those of submission that everybody uses towards everybody else.

Once the hierarchical structure has disappeared people are no longer trained in the use of its signals. Consequently the familiarity with them is lost. This, together with the ever-increasing repression of homosexuality both in its erotic and its aggressive dimensions, makes for an inevitable weakening in connection between conscious life and the unconscious, where the sexually structured patterns of dominance–submission still exist, influential and ready for action regardless of any changes of custom.

The consequences of this are clearly demonstrable. I have given a number of examples showing how men, disturbed by nervous states and feeling powerless in some measure because of them, express these feelings by sexual symbolism whether their disturbances lie primarily within the sexual sphere or outside it. Also I have demonstrated how fear of submission in relation to the doctor comes to the fore in the apparently sexual language of mounting–presentation symbols. Consequently a homosexual manifestation on the part of the patient, in a dream or in his emotional attitude, may be a signal of capitulation, to ward off an imagined danger or, on the contrary, may be an attempt on the part of the patient to assert himself towards the doctor. A manifestation of this kind may have its origins at a considerable distance from the erotic sphere in spite of its sexual form. It is important for any therapist to be aware of this during the treatment of male patients.

Repression of everything homosexual also has a number of effects on men who are not patients. Suppression of one radical easily spreads to others. So, paradoxically, the massive homosexual repression may well contribute to the fact that the level of heterosexual activity is so relatively low in our Western world — intercourse one to three times a week is a common rate — as compared to a number of other cultures where it is the rule for men to celebrate coitus several times a day. The monogamous imperative, characteristic of our way of life, probably plays its part too in this connection. In short, these two restrictions on possible sexual activity may well make for a general reduction of man's potency.

Homosexual repression shows itself in other ways too. Over a number of years it has been found frequently that inverse homosexual men, having made overtures towards young men, have been subjected to relatively uninhibited violence on the part of the youth. Such incidents have even been known to end in manslaughter. Usually the young assailant has had considerable backing in the attitude of the public. In many cases the young man reacts as he does because the inverse man's approach to him starts off reverberations from his own repressed homosexuality. We do not always have a firm control on what is repressed, and where there is inner conflict this may have unpredictable effects. The young man may get a vague feeling that by his invitation the inverse homosexual is hinting that he, too, is an inverse homosexual, and he may react with violence to this supposed insinuation, feeling himself accused of being *argr*. Of course such violence may also be no more than a cynical discharge of aggression by a psychopathic youth.

Wherever there is repression (meaning that people have lost the intimate knowledge of a part of their own nature) mistaken ideas — even delusions — may exist in conscious minds. An

N

example of this is the current misconception that children and adolescents who are interfered with sexually by grown men may have their sexual development diverted from its normal course. Another example, connected with homosexual offences, is the widespread belief that through seduction a boy may be turned into an inverted homosexual, so that he becomes fixated in feelings of attraction to men while averting himself in disgust from women. This belief is entirely unfounded. As has been shown, other cultures in the past and present abound with examples of pederastic relationships between men who are, and boys who become, heterosexual. And no cases are known where inversion may be traced back to seduction with any degree of probability. Neither do inverse homosexuals ever attempt to explain their particular way of life on such grounds. The group of boys and youths who show the greatest homosexual activity, male prostitutes, are not inverse homosexuals, nor do they become so later in life. All in all it should be stressed that no parents need fear for the future development of their boy because it comes to light that he is involved in sexual relations with other boys or older males.

Another common misconception is that boys may be corrupted morally in a general sense through homosexual relationships. Paiderasty may be used in the service of education, whether for good or for ill; so that if homosexuals were 'morally depraved' compared to the rest of the population, then there would indeed be reason for concern whenever a young person came under the influence of a homosexual. However, homosexuals are not an asocial group. On the contrary, the crime rate is probably lower among them than in the population at large, and many of them have a high standing ethically and culturally. In fact, young people have been known to receive valuable stimulus in their general development from inverse adults with whom they have had relationships.

Young males who prostitute themselves to homosexuals often

fail in later life—though, as already mentioned, they do not become inverse homosexuals—and follow a criminal career. It has been concluded from this fact that homosexual relationships have a criminalizing effect. However, this is not a legitimate conclusion. A great number of the young men were already criminals before they became prostitutes.

In this book I have tried to show that both erotic and aggressive forces express themselves through the sexual organs and through sexual patterns of action. I have chosen examples therefore which allow the erotic and the aggressive aspects to be described separately. However, as must have been apparent, quite often this could be done only when extreme cases were chosen. In most cases we see mixtures or syntheses of the two components —syntheses in which both components are discernible, but with no sharp dividing line between them. Let us take Dorian paiderasty, for instance. The two partners are tied together by the bonds of Eros, and the differences in age, development, skill and knowledge make it natural for the young man to assume the subordinate position, submitting to the authority of the older man. This paiderastic relationship exhibits the synthesis of Eros (expressed emotionally and sensually) and a relation determined by dominance–submission. The older partner achieves satisfaction of both his urge for dominance—an aggressive discharge —and his wish to love and to give—which is erotism. The boy on his part is given an opportunity to satisfy his need for submission, for being dominated by one whom he loves, admires and respects, one with whom he can be receptive.

With the advent of Christianity the genital component of the teacher–pupil relationship had to disappear. Nevertheless, on a purely emotional level, possibilities of erotic discharge remained (though they were not thought of as erotic) between the pupil and the beloved, respected and admired teacher; while at the same time the relation preserved its hierarchical character, based on authority on the part of the teacher and submission on that of the pupil.

Two radicals—homosexuality and hierarchical structure—have formed central themes in this book. The fundamental human tendency to establish a hierarchy has been well described by Lauriston Sharp. Speaking of the tribes of Central Australia, he makes the following concise comment on primitive peoples in general: ' ... every active individual relationship, at least between males, involves a definite and accepted superiority and inferiority ... Even in distant relationships there is always present a recognized element of superordination and subordination.'[6] (Note the expression, 'at least between males'.)

This was also true of Europe until the Renaissance. Thereafter the system of rank and station began to lose its hold, and during the last two hundred years deliberate efforts have been made everywhere to abolish the differences between individuals and classes and establish a general equality. We have gone far in this respect. There is surely not one of us who cannot list a series of important advantages thus gained: first of all freedom for the individual. In principle nobody is forced into a position of bondage by anybody else, all are free to be mobile not only geographically but also economically and socially—it is possible for anyone to acquire influence and to make his way according to his own choice and ability, upwards or downwards through the social strata. There is freedom of opinion and speech, freedom to choose one's occupation, one's spouse, freedom to dissolve one's marriage, and finally freedom to exert political influence by secret vote—in short the possibility exists of individual expression for all members of society in a multiplicity of dimensions.

This is all expressive of far-reaching changes in the modes and conditions of life of the peoples of Europe and America. It is also intimately connected with the abolition of hierarchy as an important structuring principle of society. What has been won, we know. However, it might now be reasonable to consider the cost also. It would be strange if the old patterns of life—patterns which have been fundamental to our societies from time immemorial—could be exchanged with no adverse effect whatsoever. Moreover this shift away from the old customs to new ones inescapably leads to the repression from consciousness of hitherto manifest radicals like that of man's affinity for a hierarchically organized social system—there would be no freedom in the modern sense otherwise—while at the same time this radical does not evaporate, but continues its existence in the unconscious and retains its reaction potential.

Usually gains are attained at some expense and some risk. It is clearly impossible to take a stand or indeed form any conviction on as recent a development as that which began during the last two hundred years and which is still in progress. It is possible, nevertheless, to point tentatively towards some circumstances and to try and indicate certain perspectives.

In her thorough description of Japanese society before the second world war Ruth Benedict[7] stresses the degree to which hierarchical systems were the organizing principles of family life and of society as a whole. Hierarchical order ruled everywhere: everybody had his superiors, his equals, and his subordinates, and everybody knew his exact station. All behaviour was attuned to this. Life was strictly regulated, stylized and ceremonialized. Most important, it was considered a virtue to 'know one's station' and to keep to it. In complete contrast to our own feeling, it was seen as a fault to endeavour to rise above one's place in the hierarchy. Naturally this ancient and strictly kept order placed great demands upon the individual in respect to his ability to forgo much and accept restrictions and tolerate frustration—or so we see it, at least. This would apply to people on every rung of the ladder from the top to the bottom. In return this system guaranteed considerable stability and security in social intercourse. Each person knew the standard of conduct expected of him and was trained to have control of his emotions according to given patterns.

During recent years I have interviewed Japanese psychiatrists about the similarities and differences between psychiatric conditions in Japan and in Europe and North America. Their opinion was that the classical psychoses—schizophrenia and manic-depressive psychosis—appeared in Japan in very much the same way as in the West. They then mentioned spontaneously a nervous, non-psychotic state which occurs frequently in the West, called anxiety neurosis or anxiety hysteria, the most prominent symptoms of which are fits of panicky anxiety, palpitation and pains in the region of the heart. This neurosis, they said, had been unknown in Japan before the last world war, but since then cases had been appearing in great and ever increasing numbers.

When I asked them for possible explanations they answered unhesitatingly that the occurrence of these neurotic states was the outcome of the immense and pervasive changes in the forms of family life and the structure of society which had been forced abruptly upon the Japanese after the war and which accorded with Western democratic models. The sudden breaking down of the rigid hierarchy provided freedom for the individual, but simultaneously he lost the security inherent in the old and trusted system with its restrictions and its protectiveness ('The Japanese are dependent people,' the psychiatrists told me), and anxiety ensued.

This could be formulated in more theoretical terms as follows: a stable and firm system based on dominance–submission, such as the old Japanese one, provides certain, well-known means of dealing with aggression. Without it the individual is left at a loss when faced with his own aggressive impulses—spontaneous aggression, aggressive reactions to frustration and so on—now released from old bonds. In such a situation, persons become prone to inner conflict, which is again apt to provoke anxiety.

In Denmark fifty years ago cases of anxiety neurosis were rare. Now neurotic anxiety is a frequent occurrence. Clinically the fact has been well documented that neurotic anxiety symptoms appear in persons who have difficulties in dealing with their own aggression. Therefore they react with unrealistic anxiety, shame and guilt when exposed to aggressive provocation by their fellow men even if this keeps within the limits of generally accepted behaviour. It is worth considering whether the situation in Japan is merely a more acute version of something which has been happening in Denmark over a longer period of time during the more gradual process of democratization there. The increase in the number of people suffering from nervous conditions which seems to have occurred over the course of this century might then be regarded as the cost—which it is to be hoped will be transitory—which we have to pay for the radical changes in our living conditions, caused by the disappearance of relationships based on dominance–submission. Nervous symptoms in a population in which most agree that nearly all are 'nervous' and 'stressed' would be a sign of more widespread troubles of a similar nature, though not so pronounced as to call for a visit to the doctor.

The changes in our society are also having their effect on education, for here, too, exception is taken in many quarters to the dominance–submission of the teacher–pupil relationship. We seem to be heading towards a learning situation freed of all personal dependence on the part of the pupil. Perhaps simple skills like stenography can be learned in this way. But when it comes to the understanding of material and the ability to use it; to the acquisition of highly organized skills in crafts, art, scholarship and science; to the ways of dealing with other people, of communicating with patients for instance, or conducting psychotherapy—to mention only a few examples—then an impersonal relationship with the teacher is not enough. In every educative process the teacher has to play the role of the model in some measure. Identification with the teacher is necessary to the learning process on any higher level, whether you are a small child or a grown person. However, as soon as identification is involved, old radicals immediately enter the scene. From my own personal experiences as a pupil and later as a teacher of adults, I am deeply convinced that you can learn nothing of real importance without putting yourself in a state of submission in relation to the teacher. Be that as it may, it is a fact, that at present our civilization is faced with the task of finding ways to deal with old, indelible, radical patterns which have lost their usefulness and are now unwanted.

In the relationship between the older and the younger generations this has made itself felt very markedly. In earlier times this relationship was given form by the exercise of authority on the one hand and by submission on the other. It may be hard to establish the causes of the recent changes, whether to ascribe them primarily to an alteration in the attitude of the older generation or to the revolt of the young; or whether perhaps a combination of these two factors is the outcome of deeper underlying changes in the groundwork of our society.

Whatever the explanation of the development, distance is inevitably established between old and young when even non-sensual, tempered expressions of emotion are expelled from their relations. The destroying of the authority-subordination relationship tends to have a similar effect, paradoxical as that may sound. Mutual 'alienation' resulting in hostility may well follow when the older people no longer possess the courage and the power to exercise authority, and the young ones will not or dare not submit. We are still waiting for solutions to this problem. Parallel difficulties, as yet unsolved, exist around the demands of employees for a voice in the management of their firms. In short, the whole question of the relations between leaders and staff is up for revision.

Let me now extrapolate from the historical events of the past and put forward, hesitantly, a possible and frightening future political development. No sooner had the Ionian Greeks of the seventh and sixth century B.C. overturned the ruling nobility than they submitted to the tyrants. When the burghers of Copenhagen in 1660 deposed the long-established and powerful board of noble councillors to the king, these same burghers instantly submitted to the king as an absolute ruler, thereby introducing hereditary absolutism into Denmark–Norway. When the French had guillotined their absolute ruler, the king, they gathered enthusiastically under the dictatorship of Napoleon Bonaparte, and so forth. Tyrants like Periander of Corinth or Peisistratus of Athens were eminent rulers indeed and popular with the people — and we know now that in many respects absolutism proved an excellent kind of government. But we want neither tyrants nor absolute rulers for ourselves. Consider being ruled by a Napoleon or one of the many other discouraging specimens who will spring readily to mind without any prompting from me. The risk is obvious: that the young 'rebels' whom today we see using entirely undemocratic methods in their combat with authority, may one day veer round and use their violent methods to elevate to power 'the strong man', the dictator, as a substitute for the authorities whom they have finally deposed.

Although considered in another context it must be dangers such as these that E. R. Dodds has in mind when, speaking of Hellenism, he states that we ourselves have observed ' ... the steadily growing mass adulation of dictators, kings, and, in default of either, athletes. When the old gods withdraw, the empty thrones cry out for a successor, and with good management, or even without management, almost any perishable bag of bones may be hoisted into the vacant seat.'[8]

Few people have sufficient strength of personality to suppress and control impulses in the long term without having recourse to repression of the disturbing impulses. Aggression, phallic symbolism, homosexuality and hierarchical order are intimately

interconnected. Therefore their conscious representations collect-
ively become suppressed and repressed, or pull each other into
the unconscious. Thus we are faced with difficulties for the individual and for society as a whole.

I mentioned in the introduction to this book that the repressions
operating in the European–North American mind of today leave
us with a narrowed field of consciousness. We have lost our
knowledge of many of the important elements of our mental
world, many of its symbols, for instance, although these symbols
still exist below the threshold of consciousness. There they fulfil
their roles as condensed expressions of the one in the manifold,
as mediators between meanings which to the rational intellect
seem contradictory and incompatible. There, too, they play an
important part in the individual's inward management of himself
—and from there they give expression to the world around them
and participate in the interplay between people.

At one time they were so real and familiar that people found it
natural to give to many of them the names of gods. Symbols and
their representations constitute the basic patterns in all cults.
The more familiar with his inner world a human being is, the
more real are the symbols and their representations to him, and
the more intimately is the religious cult interwoven with the
vitally important events of the day and year. Culture in its true
sense depends on a flexible balance in the interplay of events in
people's inner and outer worlds. Conversely the cult—and the
culture—lose their meaning when the familiarity with symbols
disappears and, with it, the feelings and possibilities of action
attached to them. At best there remains a set of fairly good
manners, humanistic ideals, habits of hygiene and technical
conveniences that may reasonably be named civilization.

As a consequence of this development in our society we are
increasingly preoccupied with objects and anything that may be
perceived through the sense-organs. (We know of no organs for

the perception of mental phenomena like symbolic images and the emotions connected with them. They are perceived 'directly'.) Philosophically the cultivation of the world of the senses is formulated in materialism, and in the natural sciences it is systematized in positivism.

It was probably during the transition from the eighteenth to the nineteenth century, at the time of the Romantic reaction against the intellectualism of the preceding Age of Enlightenment, that the narrowing of the range of human experience first became a focus for attention. The Romantics deliberately tried to recover their lost understanding of the world of symbols; they turned their gaze inwards towards the imagery of the soul, they searched the feelings, cultivating 'sentimentalism', and they believed that there existed an inner connection between the seemingly scattered and multiple phenomena of the world.

Later in the nineteenth century, Sidney Lanier—an American poet from the South who died in the 1880s—gave direct expression to his feeling that outside the boundaries of his consciousness, within his soul, there existed and moved things of which he dearly wished to gain knowledge. At the end of his poem *The Marshes of Glynn* he says:

And now from the Vast of the Lord will the waters of sleep
Roll in on the souls of men,
But who will reveal to our waking ken
The forms that swim and the shapes that creep
Under the waters of sleep?
And I would I could know what swimmeth below when the tide
    comes in
On the length and the breadth of the marvellous marshes of
    Glynn.

Soon after, Freud appeared and brought the first answers to Lanier's questions. As a result of his accomplishments and the guide-lines he provided for others who followed him, considerable headway has been made in enlarging our understanding of human nature. In practice this has proved useful in the work with patients in need of psychological treatment. But lost culture is hardly to be recovered that way.

NOTES

1. C. S. Lewis, *The Allegory of Love* (New York, 1958), pp. 9–10. First published in 1936.
2. William Shakespeare, *Othello*, III. iii. 414–27.
3. *Hávamál*, stanza 47.
4. Thomas Mann, *Death in Venice*. First published in German as *Der Tod in Venedig* (1911).
5. Anthony Sampson, *Anatomy of Britain Today* (London, 1965), p. 23.
6. Quoted from R. M. and C. H. Berndt, *The World of the First Australians* (London, 1964), pp. 80, 81.
7. Ruth Benedict, *The Chrysanthemum and the Sword* (Boston, 1967).
8. E. R. Dodds, *The Greeks and the Irrational* (Boston, 1957), p. 242. First published 1951.

Index

1. Attic black-figure vase, *c.* 550 B.C. (Page 25)

2. Athenian mixing-bowl depicting Ganymede, early fifth century B.C. (Page 28)

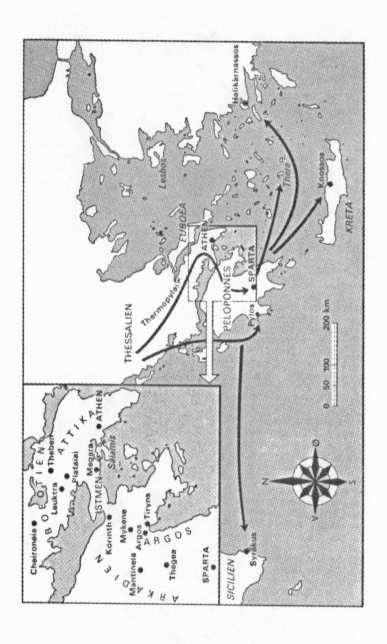

3. Map of Hellas. The arrows show the migrations of the Dorians (Page 33)

4. Drinking-vessel, showing a sculptor carving a *herma*. The inscription reads *Hiparchos kalós* – Hiparchus is handsome. Signed by the painter Epiktetus (Page 59)

5. Vase painting showing Dionysian procession with a phallic pole, sixth century B.C. (Page 61)

6. Horned and phallic god from Mohenjo-Daro, India, second millennium B.C. (Page 62)

7. (*facing page*) Stone Age cave painting from Fourneau de Diable, Dordogne, showing a phallic dancer clad in the horned skin of an animal (Page 62)

9. Stone Age petroglyph, Bardal, Norway (Page 82)

8. (*facing page*) Wall painting from an Etruscan tomb at Tarquinia, Italy, sixth century B.C. (Page 63)

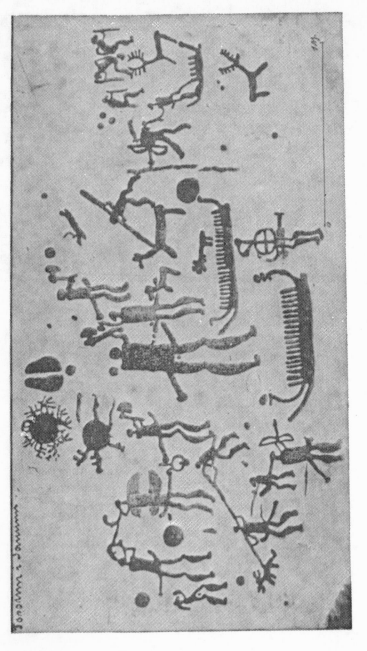

10. (*above*) Bronze Age petroglyph, Bohuslen, Sweden (Page 82)

11. (*below left*) Bronze Age petroglyph, Bohuslen, Sweden (Page 82)

12. (*below right*) Bronze Age petroglyph of 'The Sacred Marriage', Bohuslen, Sweden (Page 82)

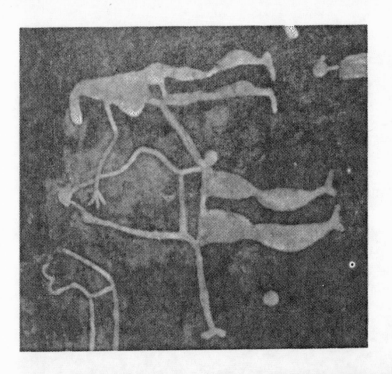

13. Bronze Age petroglyph, Skaane, Sweden (Page 83)

14. Bauta-stone, Gudhjem, Bornholm, Denmark (Page 84)

15. Phallic statuette of a god, probably Frey, eleventh century A.D., from Rällinge, Sweden, in the Statens Historiska Museet, Stockholm (Page 85)

(vii) The trial scene in Joan. Poor Joan, I was thinking of her as a person, not as a moral lesson. The pain meant more to her than the example. You instance my night in Deraa. Well, I'm always afraid of being hurt: & to me, while I live, the force of that night will lie in the agony which broke me, & made me surrender. It's the individual view. You can't share it.

About that night. I shouldn't tell you, because decent men don't talk about such things. I wanted to put it plain in the book, & wrestled for days with my self-respect .... which wouldn't, hasn't, let me. For fear of being hurt, or rather to earn five minutes respite from a pain which drove me mad, I gave away the only possession we are born into the world with — our bodily integrity. It's an unforgivable matter, an irrecoverable position: and it's that which has made me forswear decent living, & the source of my not-contemptible wits & talents.

You may call this morbid: but think of the offence, & the intensity of my brooding over it for these years. It will hang about me while I live, & afterwards if our personality survives. Consider wandering among this decent ghosts hereafter, crying "Unclean, Unclean!"

16. Facsimile letter from T. E. Lawrence to Mrs George Bernard Shaw, March 26th, 1924, reproduced in the *Sunday Times*, June 9th, 1968 (Page 105)

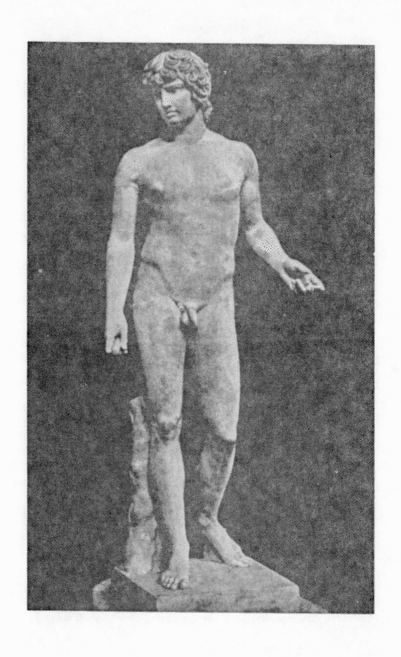

17. Statue of Antinous in the National Museum, Naples (Page 127)

18. Fragment of an Attic drinking-vessel, signed by the painter Nearchus, second quarter of sixth century B.C., in the National Museum, Athens (Page 136)

19. Attic vase showing Dionysus clad in a long garment surrounded by naked satyrs (Page 135)

20. Romanesque granite phallus in Tømmerby church, Denmark, twelfth century A.D. (Page 143)

21. The apse of Tømmerby church, showing the granite phallus (Figure 20) in its original position before it was moved to the porch of the church in 1934 (Page 143)

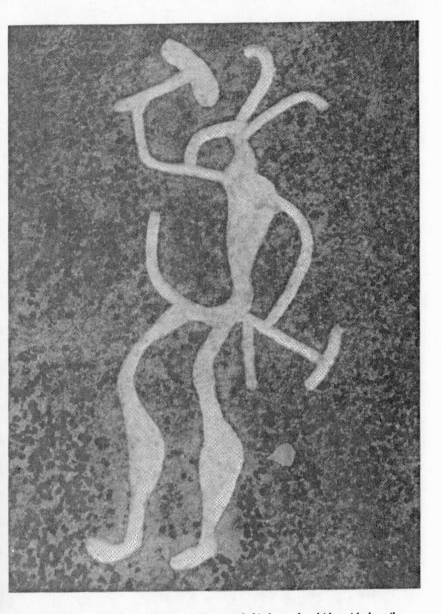

24. Bronze Age petroglyph, showing a phallic man clad in horned ox hide, with the tail hanging down and sword projecting backwards, Bohuslen, Sweden (Page 163)

22. (*top left*) A horned, phallic devil, Robin Goodfellow, surrounded by twelve witches. Frontispiece from an early seventeenth-century ballad, 'The mad merry pranks of Robin Goodfellow' (Page 159)

23. (*bottom left*) A baboon guardsman, straddling and exhibiting his penis (Page 73)

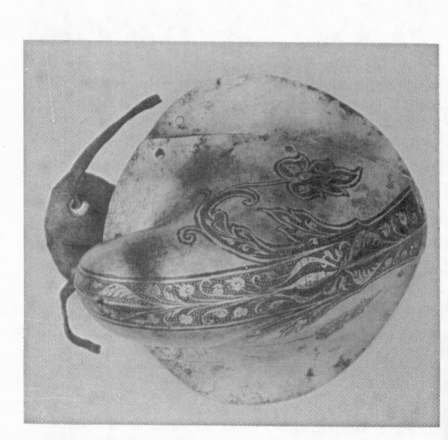

25. Cod-piece from a sixteenth-century suit of armour (Page 165)

26. (below) Bronze Age petroglyph, Bohuslen, Sweden (Page 179)

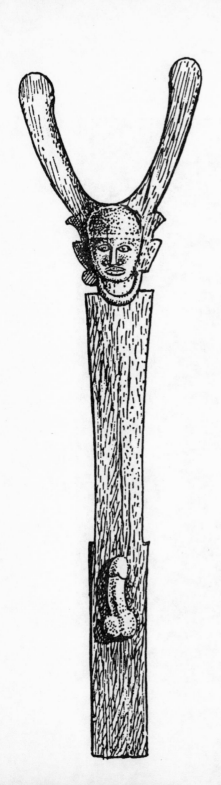

27. *Herma* from Nias in the Pacific
(Page 59)